Frances M. Bullock
110 Waverly Ave.
Syracuse N.Y.

THOUGHT AND ITS EXPRESSION

A COURSE IN THINKING AND WRITING FOR COLLEGE STUDENTS

by

GEORGE CARPENTER CLANCY

PROFESSOR OF ENGLISH AND HEAD OF THE ENGLISH
DEPARTMENT, BELOIT COLLEGE

NEW YORK
HARCOURT, BRACE AND COMPANY

PE1417
.C6

PRINTED IN THE U. S. A. BY
QUINN & BODEN COMPANY, INC·
RAHWAY, N. J.

PREFACE

This book is designed to meet the needs of college English composition courses for a semester. It is based upon the conviction, which is set forth more fully in the Foreword, that there can be no technique of form without adequate substance of matter. Many a composition course has died, to all effects, of sheer inanition, before it is half over, as teacher and pupil have sought vainly to pluck ideas for themes out of the thin air. I have attempted to supply this "substance" from the world of ideas in which thoughtful people move, and to indicate a method of using the material for composition work.

Without the kind coöperation of authors and publishers in the granting of permission to use copyrighted matter, the book could not have come into existence. For this courtesy I am very grateful. Acknowledgment is made in connection with each quotation. I am also under real obligation to Professor Norman Foerster of the University of North Carolina and Professor Robert M. Smith of Lehigh University for wise counsel and personal interest in the task which I undertook, and to my wife for constant and invaluable help.

G. C. C.

Beloit, Wisconsin
February, 1928.

FOREWORD

Thought precedes expression. There are few experiences so painful as the attempt to extract from the mind ideas which are not there. Yet if grist for the mill's grinding is at hand, mental activity once under way may be as natural a process as the playing of a child. Of course, one's thinking, under the impelling force of an idea, is not likely to be ordered and disciplined; nor does one's expression of his thought, at the moment of creative power, come forth in finished form. Revision, that secondary activity of the writer's mind, will take care of this. But the "first fine careless rapture," the glow of the mind, belong to moments of a higher experience.

Materials for the mind's working are not far to seek. Thinking begets thought, and the progeny is numerous. Analogy and contrast, acquiescence, doubt, questioning, dissent, indignation, refutation, confirmation— reactions of this sort are germinal forces in the development of ideas and their expression. Any opinion of significance, clearly stated and vigorously defended, will arrest attention and compel action in minds at all alert, and may happily stir the inert mind to life. Thought, growing in volume and power from a thousand contributing streams, will cut for itself ever widening and deepening channels, and the student, borne along by its current, finds himself entering an ampler mental life,

beside which his previous horizons seem intolerably confined. Such experience is, of course, identical with the
process of all genuine education.

The student, then, who would think and write, must
enter boldly and at once into the thought-life of his
day and generation, which is surging all about him. It is
well that he concern himself primarily with its deeper
problems, making inquiry into matters that underlie
the structure of our civilization. The little questions of
the hour need no arguing; reference to basic principles,
soundly established, is usually sufficient. But how can
one be assured that his convictions *are* sound? Most men
have an irreducible minimum of faith, a citadel which
they will defend against all comers; yet even the basic
principles, so confidently maintained, may prove to be
intrenched error. Truth is not easily arrived at; it is not
all here, or *all* there. Scholars, wise men, penetrating
thinkers, frequently hold radically opposed viewpoints.
Only the foolish and ignorant issue their pronuncia-
mentos.

The purpose of this book is to bring to the student's
consideration a number of the most significant fields
of modern thinking. Topics ever old, but new and
vibrant in these stirring years, form the basis of the
discussions. The groups of subjects constitute a sym-
posium of comment, and no viewpoint is barred, provided it is ably and sincerely set forth. The book is built
upon the conviction that the maturing student has right
of access to evidence, and that no one may fashion his
truth for him. "Education is nothing," says Heywood

Broun, "if it give a man anything less than the opportunity to choose for himself the things which he will believe." The unpardonable sins are laxity of thinking or lazy indifference, an easy jumping at conclusions, specious argument, or even, perchance, deliberate obscurantism.

For the extension of the student's reading on suggested topics, and the enlargement of his knowledge of the particular fields, bibliographical references are provided. Here will be found opportunities for further study and analysis, and material for the longer and more exhaustive papers of the course. The exercises which accompany each chapter will provide, it is hoped, suggestive material for frequent short themes and discussions.

In the soil thus prepared, it is believed that the germination of ideas will take place. Thought, discussion, the explanation and defense of one's opinion, necessitate expression. At the moment of creation, when the mind is eagerly and happily at work, the main task of composition has been accomplished. As for technique, the student who wants to write will draw to him all the agencies which are available for the perfection of his art. The wise and resourceful teacher will give helpful direction to his efforts.

A NOTE TO THE STUDENT

Since you are working to gain power in expression, you can help yourself toward the desired end in various ways. The authors quoted in this book have at their disposal, in the main, as you will see, a prose style which is clear, telling, often finely discriminating, and sometimes beautiful—as any piece of quality workmanship is beautiful. Their rich store of English words enables them to choose the term that just fits the meaning—the "inevitable word." Study the vocabulary lists with deliberate intent to enlarge your own resources, and make actual use of your newly acquired possessions.

Think of each writer as one who has commanded the attention of the intellectual class, and say to yourself: Here is a master at work; perhaps I can catch the secret of his power. Mark your book (if it is *your* book), but always neatly, as the scholar works. Underline or check phrases which are admirable because of their terseness, their picture quality, or their effective use of the concrete. Note apt quotations and allusions, flashes of wit, irony, innuendo, and sarcasm. Bits of your own comment or queries on the margin will indicate intelligent reaction to matter and manner. Be on the alert, also, to note obscurity of thought or phrasing, to detect fallacious reasoning, or an unfair presentation of a situation, problem, or group of facts.

If an article is long or the reasoning difficult, always

make a brief outline of the thought-development. The author had a plan in mind as he wrote. See if you can discover it. In this way, matter of apparent complexity will frequently surrender its meaning with surprising ease. Observe how the writer ties his ideas together, leading the reader along naturally step by step in a logical sequence. Rhetoric textbooks call this "coherence"; yet most thinkers who never sat in an English composition classroom follow the principle instinctively. It is the quality above all others that makes for good writing.

Be sure that in your reading of the various excerpts which make up the chapters you grasp firmly the particular point of view of each writer. One author believes one thing; another believes something quite different. That is where the fun comes in. Who is right? Who is partly right, who has a glimmering of the truth but does not see it clearly or in its large significance? Which author is so gloriously right that you make him your prophet?

CONTENTS

xi

CONTENTS

THOUGHT AND ITS EXPRESSION

Chapter I

THE LIFE OF THE MIND

"Style is nothing but the mere silhouette of thought," said Schopenhauer, and an obscure or bad style means a dull or confused brain. That is a fundamental and self-evident truth, and if the writer is really in earnest he will use every means to attain clear and sound thinking. To this end he will seek also to free himself from prejudice, an element subtly influential in forming the opinions of most people. The various activities of our minds have been set forth by Professor James Harvey Robinson in his thought-provoking book, *The Mind in the Making*. He finds that there are four varieties of thinking to which people are given.

OUR VARIOUS THOUGHT PROCESSES [1]

By James Harvey Robinson

We do not think enough about thinking, and much of our confusion is the result of current illusions in regard to it. Let us forget for the moment any impressions we may have derived from the philosophers, and see what seems to happen in ourselves. The first thing

[1] Reprinted by permission of and arrangement with the publishers, Harper and Brothers.

that we notice is that our thought moves with such incredible rapidity that it is almost impossible to arrest any specimen of it long enough to have a look at it. When we are offered a penny for our thoughts we always find that we have recently had so many things in mind that we can easily make a selection which will not compromise us too nakedly. On inspection we shall find that even if we are not downright ashamed of a great part of our spontaneous thinking it is far too intimate, personal, ignoble, or trivial to permit us to reveal more than a small part of it. I believe that this must be true of every one. We do not, of course, know what goes on in other people's heads. They tell us very little and we tell them very little. The spigot of speech, rarely fully opened, could never emit more than driblets of the ever renewed hogshead of thought—*noch grösser wie's Heidelberger Fass*. We find it hard to believe that other people's thoughts are as silly as our own, but they probably are.

We all appear to ourselves to be thinking all the time during our waking hours, and most of us are aware that we go on thinking while we are asleep, even more foolishly than when awake. When uninterrupted by some practical issue, we are engaged in what is now known as a *reverie*. This is our spontaneous and favorite kind of thinking. We allow our ideas to take their own course, and this course is determined by our hopes and fears, our spontaneous desires, their fulfillment or frustration; by our likes and dislikes, our loves and hates and resentments. There is nothing else anything like so interesting to ourselves as ourselves. All thought that is not more or less laboriously controlled and directed will inevitably circle about the beloved Ego. It is amusing and pathetic to observe this tendency in ourselves and in others. We learn politely and generously to overlook this truth, but if we dare to think of it, it blazes forth like the noontide sun.

The reverie or "free association of ideas" has of late become the subject of scientific research. While investigators are not yet agreed on the results, or at least on the proper interpretation to be given to them, there can be no doubt that our reveries form the chief index to our fundamental character. They are a reflection of our nature as modified by often hidden and forgotten experiences. We need not go into the matter further here, for it is only necessary to observe that the reverie is at all times a potent and in many cases an omnipotent rival to every other kind of thinking. It doubtless influences all our speculations in its persistent tendency to self-magnification and self-justification, which are its chief preoccupations, but it is the last thing to make directly or indirectly for honest increase of knowledge.[2]

[2] The poet-clergyman, John Donne, who lived in the time of James I, has given a beautifully honest picture of the doings of a saint's mind: "I throw myself down in my chamber and call in and invite God and His angels thither, and when they are there I neglect God and His angels for the noise of a fly, for the rattling of a coach, for the whining of a door. I talk on in the same posture of praying, eyes lifted up, knees bowed down, as though I prayed to God, and if God or His angels should ask me when I thought last of God in that prayer I cannot tell. Sometimes I find that I had forgot what I was about, but when I began to forget it I cannot tell. A memory of yesterday's pleasures, a fear of tomorrow's dangers, a straw under my knee, a noise in mine ear, a light

Philosophers usually talk as if such thinking did not exist or were in some way negligible. This is what makes their speculations so unreal and often worthless.

The reverie, as any one can see for himself, is frequently broken and interrupted by the necessity of a second kind of thinking. We have to make practical decisions. Shall we write a letter or no? Shall we take the subway or a bus? Shall we have dinner at seven or half-past? Shall we buy United States Rubber or a Liberty Bond? Decisions are easily distinguishable from the free flow of the reverie. Sometimes they demand a good deal of careful pondering and the recollection of pertinent facts; often, however, they are made impulsively. They are a more difficult and laborious thing than the reverie, and we resent having to "make up our mind" when we are tired, or absorbed in a congenial reverie. Weighing a decision, it should be noted, does not necessarily add anything to our knowledge, although we may, of course, seek further information before making it.

A third kind of thinking is stimulated when any one questions our beliefs and opinions. We sometimes find ourselves changing our minds without any resistance or heavy emotion, but if we are told that we are wrong we resent the imputation and harden our hearts. We are incredibly heedless in the formation of our beliefs, but find ourselves filled with an illicit passion for them when any one proposes to rob us of their companionship. It is

in mine eye, an anything, a nothing, a fancy, a chimera in my brain troubles me in my prayer."—Quoted by Robert Lynd, *The Art of Letters*, pp. 46-47.

obviously not the ideas themselves that are dear to us, but our self-esteem, which is threatened. We are by nature stubbornly pledged to defend our own from attack, whether it be our person, our family, our property, or our opinion. A United States Senator once remarked to a friend of mine that God Almighty could not make him change his mind on our Latin-American policy. We may surrender, but rarely confess ourselves vanquished. In the intellectual world, at least, peace is without victory.

Few of us take the pains to study the origin of our cherished convictions; indeed, we have a natural repugnance to so doing. We like to continue to believe what we have been accustomed to accept as true, and the resentment aroused when doubt is cast upon any of our assumptions leads us to seek every manner of excuse for clinging to them. *The result is that most of our so-called reasoning consists in finding arguments for going on believing as we already do.*

I remember years ago attending a public dinner to which the Governor of the State was bidden. The chairman explained that his Excellency could not be present for certain "good" reasons; what the "real" reasons were, the presiding officer said he would leave us to conjecture. This distinction between "good" and "real" reasons is one of the most clarifying and essential in the whole realm of thought. We can readily give what seem to us "good" reasons for being a Catholic or a Mason, a Republican or a Democrat, an adherent or opponent of the League of Nations. But the "real" reasons are usually on quite a different plane. Of course the importance of this distinction is popularly, if somewhat obscurely, recognized. The Baptist missionary is ready enough to see that the Buddhist is not such because his doctrines would bear careful inspection, but because he happened to be born in a Buddhist family in Tokio. But it would be treason to his faith to acknowledge that his own partiality for certain doctrines is due to the fact that his mother was a member of the First Baptist Church of Oak Ridge. A savage can give all sorts of reasons for his belief that it is dangerous to step on a man's shadow, and a newspaper editor can advance plenty of arguments against the Bolsheviki. But neither of them may realize why he happens to be defending his particular opinion. The "real" reasons for our beliefs are concealed from ourselves as well as from others. As we grow up we simply adopt the ideas presented to us in regard to such matters as religion, family relations, property, business, our country, and the state. We unconsciously absorb them from our environment. They are persistently whispered in our ear by the group in which we happen to live. Moreover, as Mr. Trotter has pointed out, these judgments, being the product of suggestion and not of reasoning, have the quality of perfect obviousness, so that to question them ". . . is to the believer to carry skepticism to an insane degree, and will be met by contempt, disapproval, or condemnation, according to the nature of the belief in question. When, therefore, we find ourselves entertaining an opinion about the basis of which there is a quality of feeling which tells us that to inquire into it would be absurd, obviously unnecessary, unprofitable, undesirable, bad form, or wicked, we may know that that opinion is a non-rational one, and probably, therefore, founded upon inadequate evidence." [3]

Opinions, on the other hand, which are the result of experience or of honest reasoning do not have this quality of "primary certitude." I remember when as a youth I heard a group of business men discussing the question of the immortality of the soul, I was outraged by the sentiment of doubt expressed by one of the party. As I look back now I see that I had at the time no interest in the matter, and certainly no least argument to urge in favor of the belief in which I had been reared. But neither my personal indifference to the issue, nor the fact that I had previously given it no attention, served to prevent an angry resentment when I heard *my* ideas questioned.

This spontaneous and loyal support of our preconceptions—this process of finding "good" reasons to justify our routine beliefs—is known to modern psychologists as "rationalizing"—clearly only a new name for a very ancient thing. Our "good" reasons ordinarily have no value in promoting honest enlightenment because, no matter how solemnly they may be marshaled, they are at bottom the result of personal preference or prejudice, and not of an honest desire to seek or accept new knowledge.

In our reveries we are frequently engaged in self-

[3] *Instincts of the Herd*, p. 44.

justification, for we cannot bear to think ourselves wrong, and yet have constant illustrations of our weaknesses and mistakes. So we spend much time finding fault with circumstances and the conduct of others, and shifting on to them with great ingenuity the onus of our own failures and disappointments. *Rationalizing is the self-exculpation which occurs when we feel ourselves, or our group, accused of misapprehension or error.*

The little word *my* is the most important one in all human affairs, and properly to reckon with it is the beginning of wisdom. It has the same force whether it is *my* dinner, *my* dog, and *my* house, or *my* faith, *my* country, and *my* God. We not only resent the imputation that our watch is wrong, or our car shabby, but that our conception of the canals of Mars, of the pronunciation of "Epictetus," of the medicinal value of salicine, or the date of Sargon I, are subject to revision.

Philosophers, scholars, and men of science exhibit a common sensitiveness in all decisions in which their *amour propre* is involved. Thousands of argumentative works have been written to vent a grudge. However stately their reasoning, it may be nothing but rationalizing, stimulated by the most commonplace of all motives. A history of philosophy and theology could be written in terms of grouches, wounded pride, and aversions, and it would be far more instructive than the usual treatment of these themes. Sometimes, under Providence, the lowly impulse of resentment leads to great achievements. Milton wrote his treatise on divorce as a result of his troubles with his seventeen-year-old wife, and when he was accused of being the leading spirit in a new sect, the Divorcers, he wrote his noble *Areopagitica* to prove his right to say what he thought fit, and incidentally to establish the advantage of a free press in the promotion of Truth.

All mankind, high and low, thinks in all the ways which have been described. The reverie goes on all the time not only in the mind of the mill hand and the Broadway flapper, but equally in weighty judges and godly bishops. It has gone on in all the philosophers, scientists, poets, and theologians that have ever lived. Aristotle's most abstruse speculations were doubtless tempered by highly irrelevant reflections. He is reported to have had very thin legs and small eyes, for which he doubtless had to find excuses, and he was wont to indulge in very conspicuous dress and rings and was accustomed to arrange his hair carefully.[4] Diogenes the Cynic exhibited the impudence of a touchy soul. His tub was his distinction. Tennyson in beginning his "Maud" could not forget his chagrin over losing his patrimony years before as the result of an unhappy investment in the Patent Decorative Carving Company. These facts are not recalled here as a gratuitous disparagement of the truly great, but to insure a full realization of the tremendous competition which all really exacting thought has to face, even in the minds of the most highly endowed mortals.

And now the astonishing and perturbing suspicion

[4] Diogenes Laertius, Book V.

emerges that perhaps almost all that had passed for social science, political economy, politics, and ethics in the past may be brushed aside by future generations as mainly rationalizing. John Dewey has already reached this conclusion in regard to philosophy.[5] Veblen [6] and other writers have revealed the various unperceived presuppositions of the traditional political economy, and now comes an Italian sociologist, Vilfredo Pareto, who, in his huge treatise on general sociology, devotes hundreds of pages to substantiating a similar thesis affecting all the social sciences.[7] This conclusion may be ranked by students of a hundred years hence as one of the several great discoveries of our age. It is by no means fully worked out, and it is so opposed to nature that it will be very slowly accepted by the great mass of those who consider themselves thoughtful. As a historical student I am personally fully reconciled to this newer view. Indeed, it seems to me inevitable that just as the various sciences of nature were, before the opening of the seventeenth century, largely masses of rationalizations to suit the religious sentiments of the period, so the social sciences have continued even to our own day to be rationalizations of uncritically accepted beliefs and customs.

---

[5] *Reconstruction in Philosophy.*

[6] *The Place of Science in Modern Civilization.*

[7] *Traité de Sociologie Générale, passim.* The author's term *derivations* seems to be his precise way of expressing what we have called the "good" reasons, and his *résidus* correspond to the "real" reasons. He well says, *L'homme éprouve le besoin de raissoner, et en outre d'étendre un voile sur ses instincts et sur ses sentiments*—hence, rationalization (p. 788). His aim is to reduce sociology to the "real" reasons (p. 791).

It will be apparent as we proceed that the fact that an idea is ancient and that it has been widely received is no argument in its favor, but should immediately suggest the necessity of carefully testing it as a probable instance of rationalization.

This brings us to another kind of thinking which can fairly easily be distinguished from the three kinds described above. It has not the usual qualities of the reverie, for it does not hover about our personal complacencies and humiliations. It is not made up of the homely decisions forced upon us by everyday needs, when we review our little stock of existing information, consult our conventional preferences and obligations, and make a choice of action. It is not the defense of our own cherished beliefs and prejudices just because they are our own—mere plausible excuses for remaining of the same mind. On the contrary, it is that peculiar species of thought which leads us to *change* our mind.

It is this kind of thought that has raised man from his pristine subsavage ignorance and squalor to the degree of knowledge and comfort which he now possesses. On his capacity to continue and greatly extend this kind of thinking depends his chance of groping his way out of the plight in which the most highly civilized peoples of the world now find themselves. In the past this type of thinking has been called Reason. But so many misapprehensions have grown up around the word that some of us have become very suspicious of it. I suggest, therefore, that we substitute a recent name and speak of "creative thought" rather than of Reason. *For this kind*

*of meditation begets knowledge, and knowledge is really
creative inasmuch as it makes things look different from
what they seemed before, and may indeed work for
their reconstruction.*

THE GENESIS OF THOUGHT

If it be true that so small a part of our thinking has
any real significance, by what means and through what
processes may one enter the world of "creative thought"
and share its vigorous and independent life? Shall not
one turn to books, the expression of other men's
thoughts, for contact with the best in the world of
ideas? Is not quickening of the mind to be found there?
Yet two thinkers of the last century look upon the reading habit as a force likely to render the mind torpid
and imitative. Their point of view is presented below.

DO BOOKS HINDER THINKING?

By Arthur Schopenhauer

Arthur Schopenhauer, who is chiefly known for his discussion of philosophical pessimism, was a German writer and
thinker of the early and middle nineteenth century. His ideas
about books, expressed with so much vigor and independence,
strike a note of nonconformity in keeping with the modern
revolt against standardization in the field of thought. The
following excerpt is from his essay, *Selbstdenken*. The trans-
lation was made by Mrs. Rudolph Dircks.

The largest library in disorder is not so useful as a
smaller but orderly one; in the same way the greatest

amount of knowledge, if it has not been worked out in
one's own mind, is of less value than a much smaller
amount that has been fully considered. For it is only
when a man combines what he knows from all sides, and
compares one truth with another, that he completely
realizes his own knowledge and gets it into his power.
A man can only think over what he knows, therefore he
should learn something; but a man only knows what he
has pondered.

A man can apply himself of his own free will to reading and learning, while he cannot to thinking. Thinking
must be kindled like a fire by a draught and sustained
by some kind of interest in the subject. This interest
may be either of a purely objective nature or it may be
merely subjective. The latter exists in matters concerning us personally, but objective interest is only to be
found in heads that think by nature, and to whom
thinking is as natural as breathing; but they are very
rare. This is why there is so little of it in most men of
learning.

The difference between the effect that thinking for
oneself and that reading has on the mind is incredibly
great; hence it is continually developing that original
difference in minds which induces one man to think and
another to read. Reading forces thoughts upon the mind
which are as foreign and heterogeneous to the bent and
mood in which it may be for the moment, as the seal is
to the wax on which it stamps its imprint. The mind
thus suffers total compulsion from without; it has first

this and then that to think about, for which it has at the time neither instinct nor liking.

On the other hand, when a man thinks for himself he follows his own impulse, which either his external surroundings or some kind of recollection has determined at the moment. His visible surroundings do not leave upon his mind *one* single definite thought as reading does, but merely supply him with material and occasion to think over what is in keeping with his nature and present mood. This is why *much* reading robs the mind of all elasticity; it is like keeping a spring under a continuous heavy weight. If a man does not want to think, the safest plan is to take up a book directly he has a spare moment.

This practice accounts for the fact that learning makes most men more stupid and foolish than they are by nature, and prevents their writings from being a success; they remain, as Pope has said,

"For ever reading, never to be read." [8]

Men of learning are those who have read the contents of books. Thinkers, geniuses, and those who have enlightened the world and furthered the race of men, are those who have made direct use of the book of the world.

Indeed, it is only a man's own fundamental thoughts that have truth and life in them. For it is these that he really and completely understands. To read the thoughts of others is like taking the remains of some one else's

[8] *Dunciad*, iii, 194.

meal, like putting on the discarded clothes of a stranger.

The thought we read is related to the thought which rises in us, as the fossilized impress of a prehistoric plant is to a plant budding out in spring.

Reading is merely a substitute for one's own thoughts. A man allows his thoughts to be put into leading-strings.

Further, many books serve only to show how many wrong paths there are, and how widely a man may stray if he allows himself to be led by them. But he who is guided by his genius, that is to say, he who thinks for himself, who thinks voluntarily and rightly, possesses the compass wherewith to find the right course. A man, therefore, should only read when the source of his own thoughts stagnates; which is often the case with the best of minds.

It is sin against the Holy Spirit to frighten away one's own original thoughts by taking up a book. It is the same as a man flying from Nature to look at a museum of dried plants, or to study a beautiful landscape in copperplate. A man at times arrives at a truth or an idea after spending much time in thinking it out for himself, linking together his various thoughts, when he might have found the same thing in a book; it is a hundred times more valuable if he has acquired it by thinking it out for himself. For it is only by his thinking it out for himself that it enters as an integral part, as a living member, into the whole system of his thought, and stands in complete and firm relation with it; that it is fundamentally understood with all its consequences, and carries the color, the shade, the impress of his own way of thinking; and comes at the very moment, just as the necessity for it is felt, and stands fast and cannot be forgotten. This is the perfect application, nay, interpretation of Goethe's

> *Was du ererbt von deinen Vätern hast*
> *Erwirb es um es zu besitzen.*

The man who thinks for himself learns the authorities for his opinions only later on, when they serve merely to strengthen both them and himself; while the book-philosopher starts from the authorities and other people's opinions, therefrom constructing a whole for himself; so that he resembles an automaton, whose composition we do not understand. The other man, the man who thinks for himself, on the other hand, is like a living man as made by nature. His mind, impregnated from without, then bears and brings forth its child. Truth that has been merely learned adheres to us like an artificial limb, a false tooth, a waxen nose, or at best like one made out of another's flesh; truth which is acquired by thinking for oneself is like a natural member: it alone really belongs to us. Here we touch upon the difference between the thinking man and the mere man of learning. Therefore the intellectual acquirements of the man who thinks for himself are like a fine painting that stands out full of life, that has its light and shade correct, the tone sustained, and perfect harmony of color. The intellectual attainments of the merely learned man, on the contrary, resemble a big palette covered with every color, at most systematically arranged, but without harmony, relation, and meaning.

Reading is thinking with some one else's head instead of one's own. But to think for oneself is to endeavor to develop a coherent whole, a system, even if it is not a strictly complete one. Nothing is more harmful than, by dint of continual reading, to strengthen the current of other people's thoughts. These thoughts, springing from different minds, belonging to different systems, bearing different colors, never flow together of themselves into a unity of thought, knowledge, insight, or conviction, but rather cram the head with a Babylonian confusion of tongues; consequently the mind becomes overcharged with them and is deprived of all clear insight and almost disorganized. This condition of things may often be discerned in many men of learning, and it makes them inferior in sound understanding, correct judgment, and practical tact to many illiterate men, who, by the aid of experience, conversation, and a little reading, have acquired a little knowledge from without and made it always subordinate to and incorporated it with their own thoughts.

The scientific *thinker* also does this to a much greater extent. Although he requires much knowledge and must read a great deal, his mind is nevertheless strong enough to overcome it all, to assimilate it, to incorporate it with the system of his thoughts, and to subordinate it to the organic relative unity of his insight, which is vast and ever growing. By this means his own thought, like the bass in an organ, always takes the lead in everything and is never deadened by other sounds, as is the case with purely antiquarian minds; where all sorts of musical passages, as it were, run into each other, and the fundamental tone is entirely lost.

The people who have spent their lives in reading and acquired their wisdom out of books resemble those who have acquired exact information of a country from the descriptions of many travelers. These people can relate a great deal about many things, but at heart they have no connected, clear, sound knowledge of the condition of the country. While those who have spent their life in thinking are like the people who have been to that country themselves; they alone really know what it is they are saying, know the subject in its entirety, and are quite at home in it. . . .

Least of all should a man for the sake of reading entirely withdraw his attention from the real world: as the impulse and temper which lead one to think for oneself proceed oftener from it than from reading; for it is the visible and real world in its primitiveness and strength that is the natural subject of the thinking mind, and is able more easily than anything else to rouse it. After these considerations it will not surprise us to find that the thinking man can easily be distinguished from the book-philosopher by his marked earnestness, directness, and originality, the personal conviction of all his thoughts and expressions; the book-philosopher, on the other hand, has everything second-hand; his ideas are like a collection of old rags obtained anyhow; he is dull and pointless, resembling a copy of a copy. His style, which is full of conventional, nay, vulgar phrases and current terms, resembles a small state where there is a circulation of foreign money because it coins none of its own. . . .

When one considers how great and how close to us the *problem of existence* is—this equivocal, tormented, fleeting, dreamlike existence—so great and so close that as soon as one perceives it, it overshadows and conceals all other problems and aims; and when one sees how all men—with a few and rare exceptions—are not clearly conscious of the problem, nay, do not even seem to see it, but trouble themselves about everything else rather than this, and live on, taking thought only for the present day and the scarcely longer span of their own personal future, while they either expressly give the problem up or are ready to agree with it, by the aid of some system of popular metaphysics, and are satisfied with this—when one, I say, reflects upon this, then may one be of the opinion that man is a *thinking being* only in a very remote sense, and not feel any special surprise at any trait of thoughtlessness or folly; but know, rather, that the intellectual outlook of the normal man indeed surpasses that of the brute—whose whole existence resembles a continual present without any consciousness of the future or the past—but not to such an extent as one is wont to suppose.

THE READING PUBLIC [9]

By MacGregor Jenkins

In his delightfully chatty little book, *The Reading Public*, from which the following excerpt is taken, Mr. MacGregor Jenkins, for many years the publisher of the *Atlantic Monthly*, records some of his adventures among those who read. The fond mother used to point with pride to her young son who always had his nose in a book, but the picture which Mr. Jenkins draws of the confirmed reader is not entirely complimentary.

This reading public is composed of many varieties of readers of widely differing tastes, but in general they can be divided into two pretty clearly defined groups —those who purchase and read books, and a vastly larger group who confine their literary activities to the consumption of magazines. For the orderly discussion of our subject let us treat the two groups separately.

Yielding once more to the scientific impulse, we can divide readers of books into three roughly defined classes that will help us to continue our discussion in an orderly fashion. They are:

The Sponge Reader.

The Sieve Reader.

The Duck-back Reader.

These classes form a pyramid, the apex the sponge reader, and the base the duck-back reader—between them the great class of sieve readers.

The sponge reader absorbs what he reads. He is not as a rule a gregarious or an attractive person, he is apt

[9] Reprinted with the permission of the author.

to have a little too much information for human nature's daily needs; but he is the stuff that scholars are made of and is the highest type of reader, if reading be regarded as anything but a time-killing operation. This group is small in number, and almost entirely ignored by authors and publishers, save the most enlightened, for the sponge reader reads fewer and better books than his fellows.

The sieve reader is more catholic in his tastes, and as he absorbs nothing, an almost infinite amount of printed matter can pass through his intellectual organism without occasioning distress. His desire to read is abnormal. This desire springs from obscure sources, but its manifestations are obvious. He becomes a walking directory of the titles and authors of hundreds of books, and at a pinch can present a very creditable appearance in literary circles. He loves the shallows and dabbles gracefully in them. He executes marvels of grace and agility on the thinnest of literary ice and comes safe ashore. In the company of sponge readers he is apt to be quiet and deferential, recognizing that in that course lies his only chance to escape detection, shrewdly guessing that profound silence can often produce the effect of even profounder wisdom. But get him among his inferiors, let him find himself by any chance in company with a group of common or garden duck-back readers, and he is in his glory.

He bristles with facts, with titles, with authors' names. He can rattle off the entire output of a popular author; he retails the gossip from the literary journals, and incidentally alludes to obscure and half-forgotten earlier performances. He thrills, he irritates, he bewilders. He is fond of relating with astonishing fidelity to detail the involved plot of a recent best-seller. I once rode from Worcester to Boston with the most pronounced type of this specimen I ever encountered. He happened to choose Mr. Nicholson's *House of a Thousand Candles*, and from the shadow of the Worcester station to his departure into the bleak twilight of the Back Bay, he gave me the entire narrative. It was a stupendous feat, and as I left him enveloped in the gloom of that underground chamber of horrors he solved the mystery. "I sell suspenders and read a book a day on the train." It is obvious that the sieve reader is the darling of the publisher's heart. It is he who keeps the best-sellers selling.

The third and by far the largest group of readers is the base of our pyramid, the old reliable duck-back. Unlike the sponge reader he does not absorb; unlike the sieve reader there is no easy access to or egress from his intellectual citadel. In fact his reading has absolutely no effect upon him at all, except to employ his hands to hold his book and his eyes to read the words.

As a rule this type of reader chooses newspapers and magazines; but many read books. I have in mind one of these readers, a very good friend of mine and a man of sense and character. I have studied his reading habits for years on the train, in his house, and at his club. It is simplicity itself. Purchase a paper, fold it conveniently, and begin at the top of the first left-hand column, read to the bottom, and continue at the top of the next. If a particular narrative breaks off at the bottom of the first column and you find yourself referred to column 3, page 6, ignore it. Quietly begin at the top of the second column on something fresh; it will all come out right in the end. You will ultimately get it all, and that is what you want.

This method has many advantages. It lends itself to absolute physical and mental rest. It uses up a prodigious amount of time that would otherwise hang heavy on your hands. It is ideal for the commuter; in fact I fancy that the commuting habit is largely responsible for the enormous increase in the ranks of the duck-backs.

They read their magazines and books with the same singleness of purpose and achieve the same results—a quiet hour of physical repose with no exactions on the brain. A real duck-back remembers nothing that he reads—titles, authors, publishers, mean nothing; but he goes on buying and reading, reading and buying, to the infinite delight and profit of author and publisher alike.

These gentlemen who sit at the literary throttle are keen observers, and they study their market like the sagacious business men that they are. For the duck-back reader they have contrived an elaborate and smooth-working machine known as the subscription book business. They employ armies of canvassers, they print tons of circulars, and make prodigious sales of books which are never read, but which ornament the center-tables and book-shelves in the houses of their self-satisfied owners.

A friend of mine once bought at a large price an elaborate set of books in which he took infinite pride. A year or two after their purchase I happened to be in his library—that was what the room was called—and having an idle five minutes, and being attracted by the glitter of the volumes, I ventured to satisfy my curiosity in regard to their contents. I took one from the shelf. I could not open it. It was as firmly sealed as if set with the most elaborate time-lock. I put it back and took down another with the same result; still a third with no better success. Then I realized what had happened. In the hasty manufacture of the volumes the gilt edges had been improperly applied, and instead of yielding easily to the opening of the volumes had made a solid coating of glue and gilding powder which made each book as solid as a brick.

I heard my host coming and hastily slipped the volume into place. In he came aglow with outdoor exercise and beaming with pride and delight in his home. "Nice books, aren't they?" he said, as he hurried me to his waiting motor. "I tell you a fellow can't get along without books." "Some cannot," I answered evasively.

THE DRUG OF READING
By Henry Seidel Canby

The belief that the reading habit is not always an unmixed good finds more recent expression in an essay by an American critic, Henry Seidel Canby, editor of the *Saturday Review of Literature*. It is taken from his book, *Definitions, Second Series*.

When the Prohibitionists have settled alcohol finally and disposed of tobacco, they should pounce upon the reading habit, for reading can be a drug. Observe men and women and even children upon any train or car. See how heads nod in dull intoxication over magazines and newspapers. The man across the aisle lifts his eyes. They roll for a moment in stupid vacancy, as some thought stirs feebly in his fuddled brain; then he drops his sight again into his intoxicant and drowns reflection in meaningless reading which he forgets as fast as he reads. Human beings, seemingly educated and apparently intelligent, will commit absurdities rather than sit still without something to read. They will pick old papers out of the dust and look at the comic strips, they will stretch across a neighbor's shoulder, they will carry a battered roll of newsprint bulged in an outside pocket, they will read the "Lost and Found" ads or Aunt Molly's Hints on Canning, or the end of a story in the last torn half of the *Saturday Evening Post*. In the old melodrama the hero used to cry: "Oh, God, let me not think!" That is what we all cry now when there is any opportunity for thinking; and instead of "Give me liquor!" raise one universal prayer for a page with print on it. The profoundest scholar, he whose picture appears in medieval manuscripts surrounded by rumpled tomes and barred away from the noises of day, read no more words in twenty-four hours than many traveling men who could not tell you by evening what it was they had read.

Perhaps if the Prohibitionists had more carefully con-

sidered the how and the why and the who of taking
alcohol, the Eighteenth Amendment would have been
deferred or modified; and we are far from proposing
a Twentieth against reading—even the three-quarters
of all available reading which is worthless in substance,
cheap and vulgar in form. For the real question is,
What would the mind be doing if it were not drugged
by reading? The stolid vacancy of the peasant brain
is not to be commended as a virtue, except by comparison with ignoble thinking. The gross unintelligence of
primitive man, soil-bound and work-bound, is not even
picturesque, and the romancers that praise the happy,
happy medieval whose brain was not corrupted with
machine-made ideas, forget the iron tyranny of superstition and convention which bound an intellect shut
off from news and free discussion. Vulgarity may be
worse than bigotry, but neither is a blessing.

And the answer seems to be that the value of reading depends upon the quality of man's imagination and
the nature of his thinking. If his mind vibrates with so
slow a rhythm that it scarcely pulsates unless aided, then
any reading is better for him than none. The fiction
addict cheaply living in the cheap stories of other lives
would be scarcely alive at all without his story. The
adenoidal errand-boy besotted by a page of comics is
better off than crouched in a corner staring at nothing.
But men and women who possess an interior world of
thinking, feeling, living, as vivid as the exterior world
of circumstances, are merely drugging themselves when
out of laziness or vicious relaxation they read on and on

into the endless padded columns of modern print where the level of what is said lies below the plane of their own intelligences. You can stop mental growth by reading just as you can further it. You can vulgarize taste as readily as improve it. You can get out of the habit of knowing yourself by too much lazy interest in knowing at third or fifth hand what other people are doing and thinking.

It would appear, then, that a new kind of intelligence test might be made from habits in reading. You may test the minimum level of your own intelligence by noting the point at which what you are reading becomes too inane even for your relaxed mood. That shows how far you can sink. Your saturation point is the moment at which your brain ceases to function in the presence of acknowledged excellence. These limits are arbitrary; but every reader should be able to apply the few simple principles laid down here with sufficient accuracy to determine whether he is drugging his mind with reading or stimulating it, whether books and papers for him at any given moment are food or slow poison.

BOOKS AND "MAN THINKING"

By Ralph Waldo Emerson

Ralph Waldo Emerson was one of America's great, untrammeled spirits. In the midst of a century given to too easy an acceptance of established thought, he asserted with vigor and high courage the right to pursue an independent way toward truth. The following excerpt is taken from "The

American Scholar," an address delivered before the Phi Beta
Kappa Society at Harvard in 1837.

The next great influence into the spirit of the scholar
is the mind of the Past—in whatever form, whether of
literature, of art, of institutions, that mind is inscribed.
Books are the best type of the influence of the past, and
perhaps we shall get at the truth—learn the amount of
this influence more conveniently—by considering their
value alone.

The theory of books is noble. The scholar of the first
age received into him the world around; brooded
thereon; gave it the new arrangement of his own mind,
and uttered it again. It came into him life; it went out
from him truth. It came to him short-lived actions; it
went out from him immortal thoughts. It came to him
business; it went from him poetry. It was dead fact;
now, it is quick thought. It can stand, and it can go.
It now endures, it now flies, it now inspires. Precisely
in proportion to the depth of mind from which it issued,
so high does it soar, so long does it sing.

Or, I might say, it depends on how far the process
had gone, of transmuting life into truth. In proportion
to the completeness of the distillation, so will the purity
and imperishableness of the product be. But none is
quite perfect. As no air-pump can by any means make
a perfect vacuum, so neither can any artist entirely exclude the conventional, the local, the perishable from his
book, or write a book of pure thought, that shall be as
efficient, in all respects, to a remote posterity, as to contemporaries, or rather to the second age. Each age, it is

found, must write its own books; or rather, each generation for the next succeeding. The books of an older
period will not fit this.

Yet hence arises a grave mischief. The sacredness
which attaches to the act of creation, the act of thought,
is transferred to the record. The poet chanting was felt
to be a divine man: henceforth the chant is divine also.
The writer was a just and wise spirit: henceforward it
is settled the book is perfect; as love of the hero cor-
rupts into worship of his statue. Instantly the book becomes noxious: the guide is a tyrant. The sluggish and
perverted mind of the multitude, slow to open to the
incursions of Reason, having once so opened, having
once received this book, stands upon it, and makes an
outcry if it is disparaged. Colleges are built on it. Books
are written on it by thinkers, not by Man Thinking;
by men of talent, that is, who start wrong, who set out
from accepted dogmas, not from their own sight of
principles. Meek young men grow up in libraries, believing it their duty to accept the views which Cicero,
which Locke, which Bacon, have given; forgetful that
Cicero, Locke, and Bacon were only young men in
libraries when they wrote these books.

Hence, instead of Man Thinking, we have the book-
worm. Hence the book-learned class, who value books as
such; not as related to nature and the human constitution, but as making a sort of Third Estate with the
world and the soul. Hence the restorers of readings, the
emendators, the bibliomaniacs of all degrees.

Books are the best of things, well used; abused, among the worst. What is the right use? What is the one end which all means go to effect? They are for nothing but to inspire. I had better never see a book than to be warped by its attraction clean out of my orbit, and made a satellite instead of a system. The one thing in the world, of value, is the active soul. This every man is entitled to; this every man contains within him, although, in almost all men, obstructed, and as yet unborn. The soul active sees absolute truth and utters truth, or creates. In this action it is genius; not the privilege of here and there a favorite, but the sound estate of every man. In its essence it is progressive. The book, the college, the school of art, the institution of any kind, stop with some past utterance of genius. This is good, say they—let us hold by this. They pin me down. They look backward and not forward. But genius looks forward: the eyes of man are set in his forehead, not in his hindhead; man hopes: genius creates. Whatever talents may be, if the man creates not, the pure efflux of the Deity is not his—cinders and smoke there may be, but not yet flame. . . .

Of course there is a portion of reading quite indispensable to a wise man. History and exact science he must learn by laborious reading. Colleges, in like manner, have their indispensable office—to teach elements. But they can only highly serve us when they aim not to drill, but to create; when they gather from far every ray of various genius to their hospitable halls, and by the concentrated fires, set the hearts of their youth on flame. Thought and knowledge are natures in which apparatus and pretension avail nothing. Gowns and pecuniary foundations, though of towns of gold, can never countervail the least sentence or syllable of wit. Forget this, and our American colleges will recede in their public importance, whilst they grow richer every year.

DISCUSSION AND THEME TOPICS

1. As you observe your friends and acquaintances and the great "average" of the American people, do you feel that Professor Robinson is right in declaring that if any one questions their beliefs and opinions they resent the imputation that they are wrong and harden their hearts, and that what is dear to them is not their beliefs but their self-esteem? Perhaps you would be willing to ask this rather embarrassing question about your own mental processes.

2. In the light of the Schopenhauer and Emerson points of view, comment upon the following statement regarding one man's experience with books: "Books set my mind going. I read a man's thought on the printed page. Then I lay the book down and begin to question: Has he the right of the matter?—and ideas come flooding in upon me. He has overstated here, misrepresented there; at this point his argument is plausible, but not sound; at that point he is finely convincing. My mind, at first apathetic, is roused to unwonted activity." Do books constitute for you the best means of awakening your mind to really vigorous thinking, or is the challenge of discussion and argument more effective?

3. If you do not find yourself in accord with Schopenhauer in his discrediting of the reading habit, write out a well-reasoned reply, pointing out fallacious elements in his attack on books.

4. What sort of books and periodicals have power to move the mind? Name some that do this for you. What au-

thors, present and past, repeatedly strike fire from all but hopelessly dull minds?

5. Have you read recently a book that has proved of particular significance in its thought-provoking qualities? Write an appreciative review of the book with emphasis upon what you regard as the source of its unusual interest and power.

6. What tests would you apply to a book that has come down to us from the past before accepting it as a source of wisdom and truth for the present age? What qualities in a book rob it of value and preclude its permanence? What qualities give it enduring significance?

7. Do books seem to you, as they seem to Arthur Christopher Benson in his well-known essay on "Books" in *From a College Window*, to be of distinct aid in the "quest after wisdom and truth and emotion" in the midst of the "impenetrability of the mystery that surrounds us"? Or do you look to life itself for the revealing experience? Where do you feel that you, personally, can turn most hopefully in your attempt to gain that philosophical perspective which enables us to see life steadily and to see it whole?

8. Make an examination of your personal mental traits, of the type of mind that you have, its strength and its weakness. Inquire into factors responsible for its particular quality. Inheritance, environment, training (or its lack), have played their parts. Show your ability to conceive your task, to gather your material, and to organize it into a well-ordered piece of exposition. Do not loiter at the beginning or along the way, but go to the heart of your topic, say what you have to say in clear English, and then stop.

9. Make a study of the thought-life of some group, your home town, your church, your dormitory or fraternity companions, your state legislature, your father's business associates, the country club of your town. What factors control their thinking, their points of view, their enthusiasms and disapprobations? Be analytical and fair in your valuations. Avoid cynicism and smartness.

10. Make the mental studies and analyses suggested by the titles below. Seek to make the essence of the character convincing by use of revealing bits of situation, action, and dialogue, as well as by direct statement.
    a. A Rationalizer Whom I Know.
    b. My Intellectual Aunt.
    c. What My Grandfather Thinks About.
    d. His Honor, the Mayor.

11. The intellectual creed of the "creative thinker." If such a one were asked to set forth in a series of propositions the principles by which he directed his thought-processes in his search for truth and avoidance of error, what sort of statement might he subscribe to?

12. Read John Galsworthy's play *Loyalties*, and write out a critical estimate of the basic thesis presented there.

13. John Erskine in his book, *The Moral Obligation to Be Intelligent*, sees no glory in stupid heroism. " 'Toll for the brave,' sings the poet for those who went down in the *Royal George*. They were brave. But he might have sung, 'Toll for the stupid' "—for brave Kempenfeld had been guilty of an inexcusable error of judgment. Do you find instances in the life about you of the same sort of blundering idealism?

14. Name three men living today whom you regard as "creative thinkers," and explain and defend your choice.

15. If you are in the mood, you may like to attempt an informal or "casual" essay on one of the topics suggested below. This is not an easy thing to do—that is, to do well. The trouble is that the harder you try, the less charming you are likely to be. Your artistic consciousness must be at work, of course, but the highest art is to conceal the fact. Spontaneity, naturalness, good humor, and a playful wit, are the qualities which lend atmosphere to this kind of writing. Lightness of touch should not preclude a basic sound sense of matter.
    a. On Being Ashamed of One's Reveries.
    b. Looking Into Other People's Minds.
    c. The "Well-Informed" Man.

SUGGESTIONS FOR MORE EXTENDED STUDY

1. Make an analytical study of John Galsworthy's *Forsyte Saga* with the purpose of showing how the author has attempted to reveal the operation of various forces in determining the direction of people's life and thought in middle-class English society.

2. Make a similar study of Thomas Hardy's *Tess of the D'Urbervilles*, pointing out how the tragic sequence of events in Tess's life was the product of forces over which she had no control. The theme of the novel is set forth in the following quotation from the third chapter, where Hardy is speaking of the children of the shiftless Durbeyfield family:

   "All these young souls were passengers in the Durbeyfield ship—entirely dependent on the judgment of the two Durbeyfield adults for their pleasures, their necessities, their health, even their existence. If the heads of the Durbeyfield household chose to sail into difficulty, disaster, starvation, disease, degradation, death, thither were these half-dozen little captives under hatches compelled to sail with them—six helpless creatures, who had never been asked if they wished for life on any terms, much less if they wished for it upon such hard conditions as were involved in being of the shiftless house of Durbeyfield. Some people would like to know whence the poet whose philosophy is in these days deemed as profound and trustworthy as his song is breezy and pure, gets his authority for speaking of 'Nature's holy plan.' " [10]

   Hardy is concerned chiefly with destiny or chance operating in people's outward lives. Is a parallel to be drawn in the thought-life? To what extent may the doctrine of determinism be applied in the field of the mind? If you were to write a novel presenting various types and casts of minds, would your thesis be that people think largely as heredity and environment dictate? There is a

[10] Reprinted with the permission of the publishers, Harper and Brothers.

chance for an interesting study here, taking your start from Professor Robinson's discussion.

3. Many studies have been made, in fiction and elsewhere, of communities, sects, and "sets" of people, of nationalities and races, dealing largely with their attitude of mind and the tenor of their thinking. If you find such a study ably presented, make a critical review of it.

4. Read H. G. Wells's *The Salvaging of Civilization*, and write a critical estimate of its central theme.

VOCABULARY LIST

frustration	automaton	addict	heterogeneous
imputation	resentment	pristine	perturbing
plausible	pecuniary	egress	incursion
torpid	substantiate	incidentally	dogma
fossilized	*amour propre*	patrimony	transmuting
irrelevant	saturation	prescribe	pronunciamento
squalor	arbitrary	obviousness	vibrant
self-exculpation	efflux	progeny	symposium
speculation	satellite	blasphemy	analogy
complacency	emendator	solicitude	refutation
equivocal	phenomena	hypothesis	obscurantism
noxious	bibliomaniac	stolid	specious
potent	bizarre	invoke	abstruse
chagrin	insoluble	inexorably	disparagement
metaphysics	perennial	preconception	fallacious
pertinent	illicit	gratuitous	

READING LIST

The list comprises the sources from which the excerpts in the text are taken, and other works bearing upon the discussion of the chapter.

James Harvey Robinson. *The Mind in the Making*. New York, 1921.

Arthur Schopenhauer. *The Art of Literature*. London, 1891; New York, 1900.

MacGregor Jenkins. *The Reading Public*. Boston, 1914.

Henry Seidel Canby. *Definitions, First Series*, New York, 1922.

——*Definitions, Second Series*, New York, 1924.

Ralph Waldo Emerson. *Essays*.

Arthur Christopher Benson. *From a College Window*. New York, 1906.

John Erskine. *The Moral Obligation to Be Intelligent*. New York, 1915.

Henry Osborne Taylor. *The Mediæval Mind*. London, 1911.

——*The Freedom of the Mind in History*. London, 1923.

John Dewey. *How We Think*. Boston, 1910.

George A. Dorsey. *Why We Behave Like Human Beings*. New York, 1925.

Chapter II

OPINION, PREJUDICE, AND THE "OPEN MIND"

We are naturally inclined to place "open-mindedness" among the virtues. It signifies to us an attitude that is tolerant, receptive, sympathetic toward dissenting opinion, free from prejudice, and amenable to reason. It means to us a fine sincerity and candor in the search for truth, a ready willingness, if necessary, to admit oneself in error. It is the opposite of bigotry. We think of it, therefore, as a wholly desirable quality. Minds must be open to new truth as it makes itself known, or there can be no hope of approaching absolute truth.

But is the "open mind" an unmixed good? There are some who doubt. It is asserted that this ready tolerance, this charity for everybody and everything, is indicative of a flabbiness of mental and moral character, an inability to conceive and defend enduring principles. In the discussion of great issues it vacillates, temporizes. It is particularly cordial to whatever is new. "Old ideas, ancient practices," it says, "are in error. Let us try, therefore, the new theory, the new social arrangement, the new religion. Perhaps we shall find a cure for human ills." It frankly omits the rigorous testing of the untried by standards deep-set in human experience.

Even assuming for the moment that open-mindedness is a mental state highly to be desired, we face another difficulty. Can such a condition of mind be attained? Only with great effort, say many thinkers, and then but imperfectly. No one can be entirely rid of the multitudinous forces which condition his thinking. Believing himself free, in reality he is an abject slave, held by the invisible shackles of heredity, environment, and herd thinking.

The question of the limits of tolerance and of the practical application of the principle is a subject of wide and constant debate. It leads at once to a consideration of the value of established critical standards, the "discipline, measure, and proportion" of the Greeks, the "inner check" in the regulation of conduct, as opposed to experimentation, the "law of impulse" of Rousseau, and opportunism. In short, the student will find himself deep in the perennially fascinating controversy of the new and the old.

TESTING ONESELF FOR PREJUDICE

The two tests [1] which follow have been devised by Mr. G. B. Watson, of Teachers College, Columbia University, and Professor E. S. Bogardus of the University of Southern California, respectively, in an effort to discover the first-feeling reaction which a person has when certain words or pictures are suggested to him. What is the atmosphere in which these words live, for *you*?

[1] Reprinted with the permission of the authors. The complete form of Test I, of which only a portion is quoted here, may be obtained from the Bureau of Publications, Teachers College, Columbia University. The tests will also be found quoted in *Harper's Magazine*, September, 1926, in an article, "Where Do We Get Our Prejudices?" by Robert L. Duffus.

TEST I

Directions: Read through the words and phrases listed below. Consider each one not more than five seconds. If it calls up a disagreeable association, cross it out. You may cross out many or few words. Work as rapidly as you can, but be sure that you cross out every word that is more annoying than pleasing, more antagonistic than appealing, more distasteful than attractive.

1. Nordic
2. Disarmament
3. Jew
4. Prince of Wales
5. Immigrant
6. Protestant
7. Pole
8. World Court
9. Ku Klux Klan
10. My country right or wrong
11. Roman Catholic
12. 100 per cent. American
13. Mohammedan
14. Socialist
15. Nationalism
16. Propaganda
17. America First
18. American Legion
19. Made in Germany
20. Pacifist
21. Monroe Doctrine
22. Defense Day
23. Foreigner
24. League of Nations
25. Japanese
26. Chinese
27. Reserve Officers' Training Corps
28. Quaker
29. West Point
30. Radical
31. Non-resistance
32. Independence of Philippines
33. Treaty of Versailles
34. War veterans
35. National Security League
36. Protective tariff
37. Turk
38. Armenian
39. Slav
40. Mexican
41. Fascisti
42. Russian
43. French
44. Italian
45. Greek Catholic
46. Irish
47. Mussolini
48. Preparedness
49. German
50. Patriot

TEST II

According to my first-feeling reactions, I should willingly admit members of each group (as a class, and not the best I have known, nor the worst members) to one or more of the relationships which I have indicated by the proper number. If you are wholly unfamiliar with any one of the groups, you need make no marks for it.

	1 To citizenship in my country	2 To my church as full members	3 To my street as neighbors	4 To my employment as fellow-workers	5 To my club as personal chums	6 To close kinship by marriage
British						
Chinese						
Czechs						
French						
Germans						
Italians						
Japanese						
Jews						
Mexicans						
Poles						
Russians						

THE INSIDE OF THE OPEN MIND [2]

By Frank Jewett Mather, Jr.

Frank Jewett Mather, Jr., Professor of Art and Archaeology at Princeton University, makes a rather embarrassing implication regarding the chronically "open" mind. The excerpt is from an article in the *Unpartizan Review*, July, 1919.

A middle-aged Reserve Ensign once had the unwonted honor of sitting at the same table with an editor of the *New Republic* and remarked of that sprightly organ, "The trouble is, you represent an irresponsible open-mindedness." It was a shock to find the observation accepted as an unqualified compliment. The irresponsible, which meant a good deal to the ensign, meant almost nothing to the editor. At the word open-mindedness he beamed like a child. The seafarer had had the bad luck not to be understood and the good luck of blundering upon the sweetest of words to a modern editor's ears. In idolizing open-mindedness of whatever sort, the editors merely echo the times. All young people regard open-mindedness as axiomatically desirable, like health or physical cleanliness. The mind cannot be too much open, or too constantly. Every wind of the Time Spirit must blow in lustily. The door of the mind must never be closed lest some worthy idea be excluded. In the words of the Apostle to the Gentiles we are to "prove all things," at least for the half minute or so between their entering and quitting our hospitably open minds.

2 Reprinted with permission of the author and the publishers, Henry Holt and Company.

It surprised the middle-aged man of the sea that so few nowadays read to the end of the Apostle's sentence. "Hold fast that which is good" seems a sentiment unhonored and almost unknown. On reflection this appeared in keeping with the ideal of unlimited openmindedness now prevailing. The notion, as is so often the case in all social estimates, is purely quantitative. Evidently, if you hold fast that which is good, you reduce the mind's capacity for entertaining novelties. Every conviction inside, perforce excludes a certain number of appeals from the outside. Thus the mind becomes less open. By acquiring a single principle, you may lose half a dozen fads. For a mind requiring the daily fillip of novelty, so uneven an exchange is unthinkable. It was doubtless for such reasons that the flattered editor of an eminently open-minded journal rejoiced in the irresponsibility attributed to him. It was the acknowledgment of his receptiveness, as the emptiness of a stomach is the guarantee of its ready response to a cocktail.

One or two similar adventures ashore set the sea-going philosopher to studying the entire technique of openmindedness. His endeavor to chart it is here given for what it may be worth. His first and very obvious discovery was that only young people and radicals of various ages were completely open-minded. This did not amaze him. He knew well enough that the mind hardens with the arteries. Very young ensigns often had amazing short cuts in navigation, which he hadn't. He knew those were the better methods, but he followed his own worse ones, as good enough for him. In short, he was middle-aged and knew he was. He was open-minded in that he was glad the time-saving computations had been invented, but close-minded in that he felt his ways good enough to last out his day. In short, he accepted with equanimity the evident fact that he was becoming a back number, and wished well to those who were superseding him. This seemed a reasonably open-minded attitude, combining as it did acknowledgment of his own limitations, and acceptance of his own past, with some appreciation of new ideas.

Some complacency was soon disturbed by the discovery that his own autumnal open-mindedness was entirely unlike the vernal sort now in vogue. It was soon seen that the open mind of youth opened only in one direction—namely, toward the present and future. Indeed the present hardly found entrance. Toward the past all generous youthful minds were tight closed, largely through ignorance, as it seemed. Nobody knew much about the past. It was covered in comprehensive disapproval as a period of "capitalistic exploitation." There was no wisdom in the world, and no justice, until a matter of two generations ago, when certain sages began to be "socially minded." This picture of the past was found to be very common. The view could be symbolized for the middle-aged mariner under the similitude of a barrel of spoiled "salt horse" bearing the terse legend "condemned." About such a metaphor, the historic sense of our youth invokes to cover some three thousand years of struggle toward civilization. There was neither admission of any achievement in the past nor any charity for its too evident shortcomings. It was simply wrong—a thing to be thrown overboard as soon as youth should get its rightful control of things. The future, on the contrary, was going to be completely bright and right. For this good reason the up-to-date mind should open only in that direction.

The point of view was clear enough to the investigator; yet he recalled that on shipboard the future did not take care of itself. It had to be planned for in the light of rising or falling barometer, direction, force and quality of the wind, currents, or reefs known or supposed to be ahead. To cope with this prosaic future of the navigator, a distinct estimate of situation and technical preparation therefor was necessary. Accordingly he began to study just what preparation open-minded youth was making for its future. He found, somewhat to his dismay, that about the only resource of youth as coming arbiter, was the universal conviction that the past was all wrong, and that the future would be all right because youth had attained the right state of mind. Generally the emphasis was on knocking things down. The taint of the past in the present was irritating to the socially minded. Clear away existing ideas and institutions, and the resultant wilderness will quickly blossom like the rose. Such seemed to be about the only discernible program. As regards the future, everybody felt competent to cope with it as it came along, not because he had any plan—few had plans, and these clashed con-

fusingly—but because he knew he was in the right state
of mind.

Some study of this right state of mind seemed indispensable for one who, not having it himself, might have
to live a matter of twenty years yet among those who
had. Apart from a frank contempt of whatever past
civilization had achieved, it came down to a boundless
hopeful curiosity. Take up with anything new, tie up
to nothing—was the actual practice. The trial marriage
of untrue minds was clearly the ideal sought for, and in
many cases successfully attained. The guide of life
seemed chiefly the expectancy that something would
turn up. Since something always does, the old difficult
problems of wisdom, duty, and happiness seemed solved
by a formula of easy and universal application. Just
what turned up was supposed to matter almost as little
as what had actually turned up in the past. It sufficed
that something should always be entering the portals of
the open mind. . . .

There once was a new and enterprising *restaurateur*
who, by hiring a well-dressed man and woman to walk
about in his glass turnstile, produced a pleasing illusion
of frequentation. Of course the gentleman and lady
who thus simulated a throng were technically inside the
restaurant once every turn, but only technically. Of
many minds this is a true symbol. Ideas never get inside
at all, but revolve and pirouette deceptively about the
portal.

What you open the mind upon may matter as much

as what you open it to. Suppose you merely open it upon a jumble of receptivities. Thus at a pinch you can be amused for a lifetime, but in the end he who is amused will be just nobody. Descartes conceived the bold idea of denying all his received convictions, thus creating a clean slate on which his new philosophy should be written. Meanwhile he had to live; so he took the sensible course of deciding to keep on as if he were a Christian and a gentleman. This temporary body of convictions he was quite willing to let go whenever he should have a new set of thoroughly grounded principles to replace the old. He plainly saw the folly of trying to live through the formation of a new philosophy, without some mental and moral provision for his todays and tomorrows. He is an example of the reasonable use of open-mindedness.

Unless there be some stock of principles, and even prejudices, there is no test for new ideas. They simply come and go. That a new idea is strong enough to supplant an old one is the very mark of its worth. This implies struggle, comparison, experience, judgment. A new idea thus adopted becomes a part of the man. One would no more discard it lightly than he would a leg or an arm. A mind replenished in this fashion becomes richer and stronger, without waiver of flexibility. With each change, the man comes nearer the truth that is his own. Each new principle has a greater validity than the one it replaces. The process becomes one of simplification, a weeding out of the less valuable. But the very condition of such a progress is that the mind should always contain something that is valued. It is the ultimate grace of a mind to be always ready to yield for cause, but the surrender has no meaning except that which it gains from the tenacity with which the ceded ground was once held. . . .

The professionally open-minded person of today is noisy, fretful, hasty, and wholly uncivilized. His fickleness he vaunts as virtue, he respects nothing but day after tomorrow. He leaps at novelty like a trout at feathers and tinsel, but like an ill-conditioned trout in August, never takes hold and hooks himself. He handles his mind like a cranky householder who is too busy ventilating his house to furnish it or keep it up.

If this kind of open-mindedness could be permanently maintained, it could be regarded with the equanimity of pity or humor. To the student of behavior it would be only one more instance of arrested development—the child mind carrying over into adult years. But the case is not so simple. The lack of interaction of a critical sort between what comes into the mind and what is already there, makes for a general instability which becomes an easy prey to a really strong impulse from without. It is the uncritically open minds that can be most completely and disastrously closed by a new evangel or heresy. Russia is paying today for two generations of intellectual hospitality in a moral vacuum. There is no safety for any one in opening his mind, unless he opens it upon something inside.

TOLERANCE AND CONVICTION

By Samuel Taylor Coleridge

More than a century ago Samuel Taylor Coleridge expressed with vigor a point of view very similar to that of Professor Mather. The quotation below is taken from *The Friend,* General Introduction, Essay XIII.

From this hint concerning toleration, we may pass by an easy transition to the, perhaps, still more interesting subject of tolerance. And here I fully coincide with Frederic H. Jacobi, that the only true spirit of tolerance consists in our conscientious toleration of each other's intolerance. Whatever pretends to be more than this, is either the unthinking cant of fashion, or the soul-poisoning narcotic of moral and religious indifference. All of us without exception, in the same mode, though not in the same degree, are necessarily subjected to the risk of mistaking positive opinions for certainty and clear insight. From this yoke we cannot free ourselves, but by ceasing to be men; and this too not in order to transcend, but to sink below, our human nature. . . .

But notwithstanding this deep conviction of our general fallibility, and the most vivid recollection of my own, I dare avow with the German philosopher, that as far as opinions, and not motives, principles, and not men, are concerned, I neither am tolerant, nor wish to be regarded as such. According to my judgment, it is mere ostentation, or a poor trick which hypocrisy plays with the cards of nonsense, when a man makes protestation of being perfectly tolerant in respect of all principles, opinions, and persuasions, those alone excepted which render the holders intolerant. For he either means to say by this, that he is utterly indifferent toward all truth, and finds nothing so insufferable as the persuasion of there being any such mighty value or importance attached to the possession of the truth as should give a marked preference to any one conviction above any other; or else he means nothing, and amuses himself with articulating the pulses of the air instead of inhaling it in the more healthful and profitable exercise of yawning. That which does not withstand, hath itself no standing place. To fill a station is to exclude or repel others—and this is not less the definition of moral than of material solidity. We live by continued acts of defense, that involve a sort of offensive warfare. But a man's principles, on which he grounds his hope and his faith, are the life of his life.

TOLERANCE [3]

By Harry Emerson Fosdick

The vigorous thinking of Harry Emerson Fosdick, one of the chief protagonists of the liberal attitude in religion today, has found frequent expression from his New York pulpit, in books, and in magazine articles. The quotation below is from his book, *Adventurous Religion*.

Anybody who has got near enough to the churches during the last few years to know with what wild and whirling words many of the followers of Jesus have been

[3] Reprinted with the permission of the author and the publishers, Harper and Brothers.

assailing one another must wonder about the present estate of tolerance among us. "Toleration in Religion— the Best Fruit of the Last Four Centuries" was one of the inscriptions chosen by President Eliot, a generation ago, for the court of honor at a world's fair. If by toleration one means that folk are no longer whipped through the streets of Boston for being Baptists or deprived of their ears because they are Quakers, we obviously have made some progress. But if by toleration one means the fine grace of tolerance, with its love of free field and fair play for divergent ideas, with its delight in independent diversities of opinion and its open-minded endeavor to understand and appreciate them, with its willingness to include in fellowship and work folk of goodwill who exhibit many varieties of mind, then toleration is at a low ebb in America.

Some of this recrudescence of intolerance, against which even the President of the United States has publicly protested, may reasonably be ascribed to war's psychological effect. Tolerance of independent opinion is no virtue in war. From the day that hostilities are declared, truth, for its own sake, is at a discount, and the standardization and massing of public opinion so that everybody will think one thing, is as important as guns and ships. To that end, by fair means or foul, propaganda unifies the nation's mind, and every one who dares to differ is treated as a pariah. That was done in all the nations during the Great War, and it is not easy to sober up from so prolonged and so complete a debauch of intolerance.

There is more to be said about the matter, however,
than this familiar, omnibus ascription of all our ills to
the late conflict. Intolerance has a long history and it
bids fair to have a prosperous future. Too many interests in human life are served by it to make it easy to
outgrow. By intolerance of other people and their opinions, men protect in comfort their sense of their own
unique superiority; they save themselves from open-
mindedness and from the consequent painful necessity
of changing their ways of thought and life; they defend their racial, religious, or class prejudices, which to
them are sweeter than the honeycomb; they confirm
their right to force their views as dogmatically as they
are able on other folk; they achieve gangway for their
pent pugnacity and, like the fabled Irishman, can freely
ask about every fight in which their views are concerned, whether it is private or whether anybody can
get in. Intolerance is an agreeable vice to its possessor.
Moreover, it produces some powerful consequences. It
was Martin Luther who said, "He who does not believe
my doctrine is sure to be damned."

Obviously, therefore, the proper way to begin a discussion of tolerance is by being tolerant of intolerance
and trying to discover what good there may be in it.
That it has driving power, supplies to its possessor persistence, obstinacy, doggedness, and fortitude, is clear.
Intolerant folk who have believed so singly in their
own opinions that they have hated all others and have
thought the holders of them damned have done some of
the most momentous business ever prosecuted on this

planet, and, in comparison with them, the mild ex-
positors of tolerance, willing to lend an ear to every
opinion under heaven, have often seemed feebly to lack
moral thews and sinews. There is virtue as well as vice in
narrowness. Men looked broadly at the heaven for many
centuries without seeing what was going on there; it
was only when they peered through the restricted slit of
a telescopic lens that they saw what was afoot in the
sky. So a certain exclusive, highly specialized, intolerant
narrowness has characterized some of the greatest
pioneers in thought and achievement. They were not, in
any ordinary sense, open-minded. They were terrific
believers in some one thing which they saw clearly,
and they often labored under the impression that any
one who did not share their thought deserved perdition.

Tolerance would better beware, therefore, lest in calling itself a virtue and lording it over its opposite vice,
it slip to a lower level even than intolerance and become
feeble indifferentism. There is more hope in the Athanasian Creed, with its damnatory clauses against all who
disagree, than in the futile sophism of neutrals to whom
all ideas look alike. A distinguished visitor at the Mosque
el Azhar in Cairo, headquarters of the most influential
university of orthodox Islam, is said to have inquired
concerning the cosmology taught there, whether they
held that the earth went about the sun or that the sun
went about the earth. "Your Excellency," said the
obliging and amiable Moslem, "on that point we are
entirely liberal—we teach both."

Granted, however, that a man does have convictions,

is inwardly and earnestly committed to ideas on whose truth he banks and causes for whose success he is sacrificially concerned, what shall be said about the amazing intolerance which today is exhibited in almost every area of American life?—the Ku Klux Klan hatred of Roman Catholics, Jews, and Negroes, the frequent and startling invasions of our constitutional guarantees of free speech, the itch for a standardized mental type, the earnest endeavor by law to impose upon everybody the moral customs of a group, the attempt to exclude evolution from the mental horizon of whole states by forbidding its teaching in the public schools, the fundamentalist passion to enforce orthodox unanimity in the churches—in a word, this general and widespread distaste for intellectual individuality and independence, and this eager desire to make up other people's minds for them. That this is one of the most remarkable phenomena of our time must be clear. It presents a serious problem to all educational agencies working for a virile national life, and, in particular, a crucial problem to religion. . . .

Nevertheless, the number of those to whom religious intolerance seems a barbarous survival is on the increase. The ascendancy of this new way of thinking will mark an unprecedented era in mankind's religious life, and the basic ideas which underlie the position of this school of tolerance are at least worth the stating.

For one thing, intolerance today is frequently not a sign of strong, but of weak faith. It is the man who is sure of his wife who is free from jealousy, and it is the man who is certain of his truth who can afford to be courteous to rival opinions. Said Milton in his *Areopagitica:* "Though all the winds of doctrine were let loose to play upon the earth, so truth be in the field, we do injuriously by licensing and prohibiting to misdoubt her strength. Let her and falsehood grapple; who ever knew truth put to the worse, in a free and open encounter?" From that day to this, trust in truth to win its own way, if given a fair statement and a free field, has become more and more a mark of the great believers. He who thinks that his gospel needs to be bolstered up by artificial enforcements, by heresy trials and excommunications, by personal discourtesy and defamation, does not really believe in the validity and power of his gospel. His reliance on the extraneous instruments of intolerance is a betrayal of his own unstable faith.

That this trust in truth, given a fair field, to make its unforced way, is not impractical idealism, the whole method of modern science makes clear. The typical scientist looks upon intolerance as intellectual sin. Open-mindedness, mental hospitality to fresh ideas, careful consideration of opposing views, willingness to keep fellowship in the same university or even in the same laboratory with those who differ—such attitudes are the scientist's *bushido,* his code of honor and his pride. Science relies on no exclusive and final creeds, no heresy trials nor excommunications to settle differences of opinion. Bad blood enough, to be sure, exists between scientists, because they are human, but it is taken for the ill-temper that it is and not for a holy method of defending truth. Here at least in one realm, and that the most influential in the modern world, the methods of intolerance have been in theory, and to a surprising degree in practice, eliminated.

But who, in consequence, would accuse scientists of having no convictions, of being feeble indifferentists and mental neutrals? As all the world knows, they are tremendous believers, whose assurance about the great outlines of truth evidentially arrived at is vigorous and creative, and who express themselves with decision and candor. Intolerance as a method of bolstering up science has been largely dispensed with, not because of invading dubiousness and indifference, but because of increasing confidence and faith.

When will the churches learn that intolerance, whether personal or ecclesiastical, is an evidence of weakness? *not secular*

THE OPEN MIND [4]

By *Nicholas Murray Butler*

Nicholas Murray Butler is president of Columbia University. The article which follows was presented first as an address on Commencement Day, June, 1915. It was published later in a volume entitled *Scholarship and Service*.

In what spirit and in what attitude of mind the problems of practical life shall be approached by men and women who have had the benefit of the discipline and the instruction of a university are matters of grave

[4] Reprinted with the permission of the publishers, Charles Scribner's Sons.

concern to those charged with the university's over-sight and direction. It is quite possible that one may be so assiduous in negligence and so skillful as to carry away from his college or university study little or nothing that will aid him to take a just, a sympathetic, and a helpful attitude toward the questions which life insistently asks. On the other hand, it is easily possible, and it should be normal and most usual, for the student to take with him from his college and university residence very much that will give him important advantage over his less fortunate fellows in estimating and in passing judgment upon men, upon tendencies, upon ideas, and upon human institutions. If he has gained from his study and discipline a mastery over method, a trained habit of withholding judgment until the evidence has been heard, a moral standard that knows instinctively the difference between right and wrong and that leads him to turn to the one as surely as it causes him to recoil from the other, then the university has furnished him well.

But granted the possession of these habits and traits, it is essential to beware of the closed mind. The closed mind is not of itself conservative or radical, destructive or constructive; it is merely a mental attitude which may be any one of these or all of them in turn. By the closed mind I mean a mind which has a fixed formula with which to reach a quick and certain answer to every new question, and a mind for which all the great issues of life are settled once for all and their settlements organized into carefully ordered dogma. To the closed mind the world is a finished product and nothing remains but its interested contemplation. The closed mind may be jostled, but it cannot have experience. The name of a notable historic family, the house of Bourbon, has passed into familiar speech with the definition of one who forgets nothing and who learns nothing. The Bourbon typifies the closed mind.

There is another type of mind equally to be shunned. To be sure, this type of mind is not closed, for, unfortunately, it is quite open at both ends. This is the type which remembers nothing and which learns nothing. To it the name of no historic family has yet been given. There is every prospect, however, that some contemporary name may, through constant association with this type of mind, yet become as distinguished and as familiar in the speech of our grandchildren as the name of the house of Bourbon is distinguished and familiar to us.

Open-mindedness is a trait greatly to be desired. It differs both from the closed mind and from the mind which consists wholly of openings. The open mind is ready to receive freely and fairly, and to estimate new facts, new ideas, new movements, new teachings, new tendencies; but while it receives these it also estimates them. It does not yield itself wholly to the new until it has assured itself that the new is also true. It does not reject that which is old and customary and usual until it is certain that it is also false or futile.

The power to estimate implies the existence of standards of worth and their application to the new experiences of the open mind. These standards are themselves the product of older and longer experiences than ours, and they form the subject-matter of the lesson which the whole past teaches the immediate present.

History offers a third dimension to the superficial area of knowledge that each individual acquires through his own experience. When one proclaims that he is not bound by any trammels of the past, he reveals the fact that he is both very young and very foolish. Such an one would, if he could, reduce himself to the intellectual level of the lower animals. He can only mean by such a declaration that he proposes to get out to discover and to explain the world of nature and of man on his own account and as if nothing had been done before him. He also jauntily assumes his own certain competence for this mighty and self-imposed task. His egotism is as magnificent as his wisdom is wanting. Such an one possesses neither an open mind nor a closed mind, but a mind open at both ends, through which a stream of sensation and feeling will pour without leaving any more permanent conscious impression than the lapping waves leave on the sandy shore.

The man of open mind, on the contrary, while keenly alive to the experiences of the present, will eagerly search the records of the past for their lessons, in order that he may be spared from trying to do over again what has once been proved useless, wasteful, or wrong. The man of open mind will watch the rise and fall of nations; the struggle of human ambition, greed, and thirst for power; the loves and hates of men and women as these have affected the march of events; the migration

of peoples; the birth, development, and application of
ideas; the records of human achievement in letters, in
the arts, and in science; the speculations and the beliefs
of man as to what lies beyond the horizon of sense, with
a view to seeking a firm foundation for the fabric of
his own knowledge and his own faith. His open-mindedness will manifest itself in hearkening to the testimony
of other men, other peoples, and other ages, as well as
in reflecting upon and weighing the evidence of his own
short-lived and very limited senses.

There is a great difference between being intellectual
and being intelligent. Not a few intellectual persons are
quite unintelligent, and very many intelligent persons
would hardly be classed as intellectual. One of the chief
manifestations of intelligence is open-mindedness. The
intelligent man is open-minded enough to see the point
of view of those who do not agree with him and to enter
in some measure into their feelings and convictions. He
is able, also, to view the conflicting arguments and phenomena in proportion to each other and to rank the less
significant of these below the more significant. It is
quite possible to be intellectual and to manifest the
closed mind: but it is not possible to do so and to be
intelligent.

It is the constant aim of this college and university,
by act and by precept, to hold up the value of open-
mindedness and to train students in ways of intelligence. This university is the product of liberty, and it is
passionately devoted to liberty. It finds in liberty the
justification and the ground for open-mindedness, and

also the source of those dangers which it is the business of the educated man to avoid. Open-mindedness in the university teaches the habit of open-mindedness in later life. Genuine open-mindedness guides to progress based upon wisdom. That each one of you may have caught something of this spirit and may constantly and effectively manifest it in the years to come is our earnest wish and hope.

THE HOSPITABLE MIND [5]

By William Lyon Phelps

The following brief excerpt is from *Scribner's Magazine*, May, 1926. Professor Phelps is a member of the English department of Yale University and a well-known literary critic.

I am not an agnostic, or a socialist, or a revolutionist, or an anarchist; but I have sufficient faith in God and the United States to believe that neither can be injured by free thought and free expression. There is no reason why the strongest religious and political convictions should not be accompanied by clear-eyed tolerance. Tolerance is the mark of the truly civilized and cultivated, mature mind. Those who are habitually intolerant can never learn, never develop; but a hospitable mind is ever growing.

[5] Reprinted with the permission of the publishers, Charles Scribner's Sons.

CHANGE AND GROWTH [6]

By Stuart Sherman

Stuart Sherman was formerly professor of English at the University of Illinois. In 1924 he became editor of "Books," the literary supplement of the New York *Herald-Tribune*. His untimely death in 1926 was a great loss to American letters. The following quotation is taken from the introduction to his last book, *Critical Woodcuts*.

It has been intimated to me that this book shows significant changes in my point of view and in my opinions. Perhaps it does. If so I trust that some reviewer, hostile to change, will go patiently through the essays, collect the evidence, compare it with previously accessible evidence, and point out my aberrations and inconsistencies. I have never taken a vow to carry any opinion unaltered to the grave; and if it can be proved tonight that I have learned absolutely nothing since morning, I shall be dismayed.

DISCUSSION AND THEME TOPICS

1. What did Dr. Samuel Johnson mean when he said of Oliver Goldsmith, "Sir, he knows nothing: he has made up his mind about nothing"? Was the criticism just?
2. Here is a bit of reported conversation. What are its implications?

   "But tell me: is there nothing which you really hate? Do you tolerate everything?"

   "Yes, I hate intolerance. I can tolerate everything but that."

   "Quibbler!" I said.
3. Write a short paper in which you comment frankly upon the showing which you made in Tests I and II, explain-

[6] *Ibid.*

ing, and if possible defending, the "first-feeling" reactions which your answers indicated.

4. Write an open letter to a local paper which represents obviously a narrow and intolerant position on some topic of public concern.

5. Write the editor's reply to this letter in an editorial appearing the following day, the editor exhibiting a sane and broad-minded intelligence.

6. Tolerance and conviction.

When do these two come into conflict? At what point, for instance, does your own intolerance begin? Compare your case with that of others, and illustrate. When a conflict of the virtues arises, what course may be pursued? Present a thoughtful discussion of the question.

7. Tolerance and the law.

Law is admittedly intolerant. Otherwise it is not law, but merely opinion. Law forces the action of others and must be obeyed. It is intolerant of dissent. When the statute goes on the books, the mind of the public crystallizes into intolerance. Is there again a conflict of the virtues?

8. Tolerance and reform.

The reformer by his very nature is intolerant, and strong in his convictions. Tolerance does not change the *status quo*; it puts up with it. The reformer is at war with things as they are, and thus the old order is overthrown. Is tolerance but one step removed from the *laissez-faire* attitude and indifferentism, and hence essentially dangerous? May not all the forward steps of civilization be found to have their origin in intolerance? Use specific instances and build up a generalization.

9. Tolerance and censorship.

Discuss some phase of the operation of censorship—for instance, in the field of drama, moving pictures, fiction, or the magazines. Explain what seems to you a sensible and enlightened procedure, based upon enduring principles.

10. Make a character study of some significant reformer of

the present or past, and show how he fits into your philosophy of "open-mindedness."

11. "To die for an idea is to attach a very high price to conjectures . . . There is a certain impertinence in letting oneself be burned for an opinion" (Anatole France, quoted by Barry Cerf in his book, *The Degeneration of a Great Artist*). Write a discussion of this declaration.

12. "I do not agree with a word that you say, but I will defend to the death your right to say it" (Voltaire, in his "Letters"). Offer comment.

SUGGESTIONS FOR MORE EXTENDED STUDY

1. Most of the topics suggested above, if treated with any fullness, may well be the subjects of long papers.

2. Prepare carefully an outline on the topic, "The Open Mind," with several main headings which indicate the chief phases of the discussion and with subheadings sufficiently full to present point by point the development of the argument. Submit the outline to your instructor for criticism. Then prepare the paper on the basis of the outline. Your discussion should express what you believe to be the residual truth in the clash between tolerance and conviction.

VOCABULARY LIST

amenable	propaganda	ascribe
multitudinous	trammels	perdition
bigotry	conjecture	residual
vacillate	sophism	articulate
temporize	vogue	protagonist
exploitation	crucial	pirouette
recrudescence	ostentation	indifferentism
pent	computation	*status quo*
aberrations	arbiter	impertinence
cant	simulate	virile
slogan	evangel	extraneous
fillip	fallibility	cosmology

terse
jauntily
laissez-faire
Athanasian Creed
agnostic
pugnacity
dogmatic

unanimity
abject
equanimity
unprecedented
axiomatically
transcend
fundamentalist

specific
pariah
omnibus
perennial
replenish
validity

READING LIST

The list comprises the sources from which the excerpts in the text are taken.

Robert L. Duffus. "Where Do We Get Our Prejudices?" *Harper's Magazine,* September, 1926.

Frank Jewett Mather. "The Inside of the Open Mind." *Unpartizan Review,* July, 1919.

Samuel Taylor Coleridge. *The Friend.* General Introduction, Essay XIII.

Harry Emerson Fosdick. *Harper's Magazine,* May, 1926.

Nicholas Murray Butler. *Scholarship and Service.* New York, 1921.

William Lyon Phelps. *Scribner's Magazine,* May, 1926.

Stuart Sherman. *Critical Woodcuts.* New York, 1926.

Chapter III

STANDARDS, TASTE, INSTINCT; THE PLACE
OF THE CRITIC

In the effort to attain to a life of intelligence and
sane perspective in the present age, one is constantly at a
loss as to where to turn to find enduring truth. What
is the essential good? Will the principles and programs
which have served a past civilization be capable of
serving a new and vastly more complex world? Where
may man confidently place his trust? Shall it be in the
primitive instinct which he shares with his fellow animals and under whose direction he gives unconsidered
obedience to the "law of impulse"? Or is there safety
in the standards which civilization has evolved from
tragic centuries of trial and error, in the controls of an
established society, and in the "inner check" of a disciplined conscience? Shall there be an exaltation of the
"natural man" and a recognition of the legitimacy of
impulse, as Rousseau and his followers have taught; or
shall the Greek ideal of "discipline, measure, and proportion" prevail?

The controversy has ramifications and bearings in
myriad aspects of our modern life. Let us look at some
approaches which various thinkers have made to the
subject.

ROUSSEAU'S LAW OF INSTINCT [1]

By Lane Cooper

Jean Jacques Rousseau, philosopher and teacher of the eighteenth century, was the brilliant exponent of instinct and impulse as trustworthy guides of conduct. The natural man is essentially good and happy; suffering and evil have come from the artificial structures of society. Professor Lane Cooper in his book *Two Views of Education* presents briefly the main point of Rousseau's teaching, as set forth in his *Emile*.

Coming from the hand of the Author of all things, contends Rousseau, the child, like every other part of creation, is good; whereas in the hands of man everything degenerates. The depravity we observe in those about us is not inborn; it arises from the first contact of the individual, a vicious contact, with his kind. From this first depravity all others come in succession; the entire moral order is changed, and natural feeling is extinguished in all hearts. Do you wish, then, that the child shall preserve his original form? Help him to preserve it from the moment he enters the world. . . . The child, in his view, is a child of God, and is therefore good. If we free his inborn tendency from hindrances, nature will do the rest. The teacher is simply the power that affords nature a chance of which nature will gladly avail itself. In general, under the scheme of Rousseau, the child is to escape censure; he is not to do anything because it is traditional; he is to live in the present, not forced to perform actions with a view to his subsequent welfare; his studies are not fixed, he is free

[1] Reprinted with the permission of the Yale University Press.

to choose what he will learn; he knows nothing of discipline. In this arrangement, obviously, to teach is to please, and to profit is to furnish entertainment. The chief end of man is present glory and enjoyment. . . .

The history of American education, as we can see by a glance at the change which occurred in the last fifty years of the nineteenth century, has meant a gradual movement away from the ideals of Calvin and the Protestant Reformation toward those of Rousseau and the French Revolution. We have come to aim less at ultimate improvement, and more at immediate satisfaction. Not discipline, but content, is the watchword. We are not to trouble ourselves and our students with what is old, difficult, unnatural, and far away, when we and they crave what is new, easy, natural, and close at hand. The chief end of man is to make a living and to adapt himself comfortably to his environment.

REASON VERSUS INSTINCT [2]

By Will Durant

Mr. Will Durant, in his absorbingly interesting *Story of Philosophy,* from which the two following passages are taken, makes clear the essential clash between intellect and instinct as represented in the position of the two men who more than any others directed the trend of eighteenth-century thought in Europe.

Yet he [Voltaire] did not quite realize what was happening about him; and he never for a moment supposed that in this "splendid outburst" all France would ac-

[2] Reprinted with the permission of the publishers, Simon and Schuster.

cept enthusiastically the philosophy of this queer Jean
Jacques Rousseau who, from Geneva and Paris, was
thrilling the world with sentimental romances and revolutionary pamphlets. The complex soul of France seems
to have divided itself into these two men, so different
and yet so French. Nietzsche speaks of *"la gaya scienza,*
the light feet, wit, fire, grace, strong logic, arrogant in-
tellectuality, the dance of the stars"—surely he was
thinking of Voltaire. Now beside Voltaire put Rousseau:
all heat and fantasy, a man with noble and jejune visions,
the idol of *la bourgeoise gentille-femme,* announcing
like Pascal that the heart has its reasons which the head
can never understand.

In these two men we see again the old clash between
intellect and instinct. Voltaire believed in reason always: "we can, by speech and pen, make men more
enlightened and better." Rousseau had little faith in
reason; he desired action; the risks of revolution did
not frighten him; he relied on the sentiment of brotherhood to reunite the social elements scattered by turmoil
and the uprooting of ancient habits. Let laws be removed, and men would pass into a reign of equality and
justice. When he sent to Voltaire his *Discourse on the
Origin of Inequality,* with its arguments against civilization, letters, and science, and for a return to the
natural conditions as seen in savages and animals, Voltaire replied: "I have received, sir, your new book
against the human species, and I thank you for it. . . .
No one has ever been so witty as you are in trying to
turn us into brutes; to read your book makes one long to

go on all fours. As, however, it is now some sixty years since I gave up the practice, I feel that it is unfortunately impossible for me to resume it." He was chagrined to see Rousseau's passion for savagery continue into the *Social Contract:* "Ah, Monsieur," he writes to M. Bordes, "you see now that Jean Jacques resembles a philosopher as a monkey resembles a man." He is the "dog of Diogenes gone mad." Yet he attacked the Swiss authorities for burning the book, holding to his famous principle: "I do not agree with a word that you say, but I will defend to the death your right to say it." And when Rousseau was fleeing from a hundred enemies Voltaire sent him a cordial invitation to come and stay with him at Les Délices. What a spectacle that would have been!

refute

Voltaire was convinced that all this denunciation of civilization was boyish nonsense; that man was incomparably better off under civilization than under savagery; he informs Rousseau that man is by nature a beast of prey, and that civilized society means a chaining of this beast, a mitigation of his brutality, and the possibility of the development, through social order, of the intellect and its joys. . . . After all, when one tries to change institutions without having changed the nature of men, that unchanged nature will soon resurrect those institutions.

Here was the old vicious circle; men form institutions, and institutions form men; where could change break into this ring? Voltaire and the liberals thought that intellect could break the ring by educating and changing men, slowly and peacefully; Rousseau and the radicals felt that the ring could be broken only by instinctive and passionate action that would break down the old institutions and build, at the dictates of the heart, new ones under which liberty, equality, and fraternity would reign. Perhaps the truth lay above the divided camps; that instinct must destroy the old, but that only intellect can build the new. . . .

Reason is no final test [was the argument of Rousseau]. There are some theoretical conclusions against which our whole being rebels; we have no reason to presume that these demands of our nature must be stifled at the dictates of a logic which is after all but the recent construction of a frail and deceptive part of us. How often our instincts and feelings push aside the little syllogisms which would like us to behave like geometrical figures, and make love with mathematical precision! Sometimes, no doubt—and particularly in the novel complexities and artificialities of urban life— reason is the better guide; but in the great crises of life, and in great problems of conduct and belief, we trust to our feelings rather than to our diagrams. If reason is against religion, so much the worse for reason!

THE HEBREW AND THE GREEK IDEALS
By Matthew Arnold

The name of Matthew Arnold has come to be identified with the Hellenism which he preached as the saving grace of existence. This Hellenism is the spirit, the attitude of mind, which informs all of Arnold's critical approach to life and literature. It stands for elevation, for quality, for a conception of life in its possible symmetry and wholeness, for an intelligent and finely discriminating analysis of values, for an openness of mind and an eagerness of spirit in the search for goodness and beauty, for "sweetness and light," for "the best that has been thought and said in the world." The enemies that he fought were narrowness, bigotry, harshness, the intolerable rule of letter rather than of spirit, cheapness and vulgarity, and ignorant self-satisfaction and crass materialism, which he termed "Philistinism." One can hardly come intelligently to the problems of our century until he is thoughtfully, if not sympathetically, aware of the program of life which this great prophet of culture attempted to set before the middle-class Englishman of the last century.

The quotation below is from Arnold's essay, "Hebraism and Hellenism," and is essentially a definition of terms. Though recognizing the complementary value of the two ways of thought here expounded, he scarcely succeeds in hiding his enthusiasm for the Greek ideal. It will be seen that both conceptions are definitely opposed to Rousseau's law of nature.

Let me go back for a moment to Bishop Wilson, who says: "First, never go against the best light you have; secondly, take care that your light be not darkness." We show, as a nation, laudable energy and persistence in walking according to the best light we have, but are not quite careful enough, perhaps, to see that our light be not darkness. This is only another version of the old story that energy is our strong point and favorable characteristic, rather than intelligence. But we may give to this idea a more general form still, in which it will have a yet larger range of application. We may regard this energy driving at practice, this paramount sense of the obligation of duty, self-control, and work, this earnestness in going manfully with the best light we have, as one force. And we may regard the intelligence driving at those ideas which are, after all, the basis of right practice, the ardent sense for all the new and changing combinations of them which man's development brings with it, the indomitable impulse to know and adjust them perfectly, as another force. And these two forces we may regard as in some sense rivals—rivals not by the necessity of their own nature, but as exhibited in man and his history—and rivals dividing the empire of the world between them. And to give these forces names from the two races of men who have supplied the most signal and splendid manifestations of them, we may call them respectively the forces of Hebraism and Hellenism. Hebraism and Hellenism—between these two points of influence moves our world. At one time it feels more powerfully the attraction of one of them, at another time of the other; and it ought to be, though it never is, evenly and happily balanced between them. . . .

The uppermost idea with Hellenism is to see things as they really are; the uppermost idea with Hebraism is conduct and obedience. Nothing can do away with this ineffaceable difference. The Greek quarrel with the body and its desires is, that they hinder right thinking; the Hebrew quarrel with them is, that they hinder right acting. "He that keepeth the law, happy is he"—"Blessed is the man that feareth the Eternal, that delighteth greatly in his commandments"—that is the Hebrew notion of felicity; and pursued with passion and tenacity, this notion would not let the Hebrew rest till, as is well known, he had at last got out of the law a network of prescriptions to enwrap his whole life, to govern every moment of it, every impulse, every action. The Greek notion of felicity, on the other hand, is perfectly conveyed in these words of a great French moralist: *C'est le bonheur des hommes*—when? when they abhor that which is evil?—no; when they exercise themselves in the law of the Lord day and night?—no; when they die daily?—no; when they walk about the New Jerusalem with palms in their hands?—no; but when they think aright, when their thought hits: *quand ils pensent juste*. . . .

To get rid of one's ignorance, to see things as they are, and by seeing them as they are to see them in their beauty, is the simple and attractive ideal which Hellenism holds out before human nature; and from the simplicity and charm of this ideal, Hellenism, and human life in the hands of Hellenism, is invested with a kind of aërial ease, clearness, and radiancy; they are full of what we call sweetness and light. Difficulties are kept out of view, and the beauty and rationalness of the ideal have all our thoughts. . . .

Hebraism—and here is the source of its wonderful strength—has always been severely preoccupied with an awful sense of the impossibility of being at ease in Zion; of the difficulties which oppose themselves to man's pursuit or attainment of that perfection of which Socrates talks so hopefully, and, as from this point of view one might almost say, so glibly. It is all very well to talk of getting rid of one's ignorance, of seeing things in their reality, seeing them in their beauty; but how is this to be done when there is something which thwarts and spoils all our efforts?

This something is *sin*; and the space which sin fills in Hebraism, as compared with Hellenism, is indeed pro- *immense* digious. This obstacle to perfection fills the whole scene, and perfection appears remote and rising away from earth, in the background. Under the name of sin, the difficulties of knowing oneself and conquering oneself which impede man's passage to perfection, become, for Hebraism, a positive, active entity hostile to man, a mysterious power which I heard Dr. Pusey the other day, in one of his impressive sermons, compare to a hideous hunchback seated on our shoulders, and which it is the main business of our lives to hate and oppose. The discipline of the Old Testament may be summed up as a discipline teaching us to abhor and flee from sin; the discipline of the New Testament, as a discipline teaching us to die to it. As Hellenism speaks of thinking clearly, seeing things in their essence and beauty, as a grand and precious feat for man to achieve, so Hebraism speaks of becoming conscious of sin, of awakening to a sense of sin, as a feat of this kind. It is obvious to what wide divergence these differing tendencies, ac- tively followed, must lead. As one passes and repasses from Hellenism to Hebraism, from Plato to St. Paul, one feels inclined to rub one's eyes and ask oneself whether man is indeed a gentle and simple being, show- ing the traces of a noble and divine nature; or an un- happy chained captive, laboring with groanings that cannot be uttered to free himself from the body of this death. . . .

Puritanism, which has been so great a power in the English nation, and in the strongest part of the English nation, was originally the reaction, in the seventeenth century, of the conscience and moral sense of our race, against the moral indifference and lax rule of conduct which in the sixteenth century came in with the Renaissance. It was a reaction of Hebraism against Hellenism; and it powerfully manifested itself, as was natural, in a people with much of what we call a Hebraizing turn, with a signal affinity for the bent which was the master-bent of Hebrew life. Eminently Indo-European by its *humor*, by the power it shows, through this gift, of imaginatively acknowledging the multiform aspects of the problem of life, and of thus getting itself unfixed from its own over-certainty, of smiling at its own over-tenacity, our race has yet (and a great part of its strength lies here), in matters of practical life and moral conduct, a strong share of the assuredness, the tenacity, the intensity of the Hebrews. This turn manifested itself in Puritanism, and has had a great part in shaping our history for the last two hundred years.

THE GLORY OF SELFHOOD
By Ralph Waldo Emerson

In Emerson's sturdy assertion of the glory of selfhood, and the worth and dignity of the individual, some have found a touch of Rousseau. Be that as it may, his essay "Self-Reliance," from which the following excerpt is taken, is a stirring declaration of the soul's independence.

I read the other day some verses written by an eminent painter which were original and not conventional. The soul always hears an admonition in such lines, let the subject be what it may. The sentiment they instill is of more value than any thought they may contain. To believe your own thought, to believe that what is true for you in your private heart is true for all men— that is genius. Speak your latent conviction, and it shall be the universal sense; for the inmost in due time becomes the outmost, and our first thought is rendered back to us by the trumpets of the Last Judgment. Familiar as the voice of the mind is to each, the highest merit we ascribe to Moses, Plato, and Milton is that they set at naught books and traditions, and spoke not what men, but what *they* thought. A man should learn to detect and watch that gleam of light which flashes across his mind from within, more than the luster of the firmament of bards and sages. Yet he dismisses without notice his thought, because it is his. In every work of genius we recognize our own rejected thoughts; they come back to us with a certain alienated majesty. Great works of art have no more affecting lesson for us than this. They teach us to abide by our spontaneous impression with good-humored inflexibility then most when the whole cry of voices is on the other side. Else tomorrow a stranger will say with masterly good sense precisely what we have thought and felt all the time, and we shall be forced to take with shame our own opinion from another. . . .

Whoso would be a man must be a nonconformist. He who would gather immortal palms must not be hindered by the name of goodness, but must explore if it be goodness. Nothing is at last sacred but the integrity of your own mind. Absolve you to yourself, and you shall have the suffrage of the world. I remember an answer which when quite young I was prompted to make to a valued adviser who was wont to importune me with the dear old doctrines of the church. On my saying, "What have I to do with the sacredness of traditions, if I live wholly from within?"—my friend suggested, "But these impulses may be from below, not from above." I replied, "They do not seem to me to be such; but if I am the devil's child, I will live then from the devil." No law can be sacred to me but that of my nature. Good and bad are but names very readily transferable to that or this; the only right is what is after my constitution; the only wrong what is against it. A man is to carry himself in the presence of all opposition as if everything were titular and ephemeral but he. I am ashamed to think how easily we capitulate to badges and names, to large societies and dead institutions. Every decent and well-spoken individual affects and sways me more than is right. I ought to go upright and vital, and speak the rude truth in all ways. If malice and vanity wear the coat of philanthropy, shall that pass? If an angry bigot assumes this bountiful cause of Abolition, and comes to me with his last news from Barbadoes, why should I not say to him, "Go love thy infant; love thy woodchopper; be good-natured and modest; have that grace; and never varnish your hard, uncharitable ambition with this incredible tenderness for black folk a thousand miles off. Thy love afar is spite at home." Rough and graceless would be such greeting, but truth is handsomer than the affectation of love. Your goodness must have some edge to it—else it is none. The doctrine of hatred must be preached, as the counteraction of the doctrine of love, when that pules and whines. I shun father and mother and wife and brother when my genius calls me. I would write on the lintels of the door-post, *Whim*. I hope it is somewhat better than whim at last, but we cannot spend the day in explanation. Expect me not to show cause why I seek or why I exclude company. Then again, do not tell me, as a good man did today, of my obligation to put all poor men in good situations. Are they *my* poor? I tell thee, thou foolish philanthropist, that I grudge the dollar, the dime, the cent I give to such men as do not belong to me and to whom I do not belong. There is a class of persons to whom by all spiritual affinity I am bought and sold; for them I will go to prison, if need be; but your miscellaneous popular charities; the education at college of fools; the building of meeting-houses to the vain end to which many now stand; alms to sots, and the thousandfold relief societies —though I confess with shame I sometimes succumb and give the dollar, it is a wicked dollar, which by-and-by I shall have the manhood to withhold. . . .

Insist on yourself; never imitate. Your own gift you

can present every moment with the cumulative force of a whole life's cultivation; but of the adopted talent of another you have only an extemporaneous half possession. That which each can do best, none but his Maker can teach him. No man yet knows what it is, nor can, till that person has exhibited it. Where is the master who could have taught Shakespeare? Where is the master who could have instructed Franklin, or Washington, or Bacon, or Newton? Every great man is a unique. The Scipionism of Scipio is precisely that part he could not borrow. Shakespeare will never be made by the study of Shakespeare. Do that which is assigned you, and you cannot hope too much or dare too much. There is at this moment for you an utterance brave and grand as that of the colossal chisel of Phidias, or trowel of the Egyptians, or the pen of Moses, or Dante, but different from all these. Not possibly will the soul, all rich, all eloquent, with thousand-cloven tongue, deign to repeat itself; but if you can hear what these patriarchs say, surely you can reply to them in the same pitch of voice; for the ear and the tongue are two organs of one nature. Abide in the simple and noble regions of thy life, obey thy heart, and thou shalt reproduce the Fore-world again.

THE LAW OF CONTROL

During the last few years there has grown up in America a group of vigorous thinkers who maintain that a blind following of instinct will lead to nothing but degradation and disaster, that civilization makes progress only through an intelligent control, or even repression, of the natural impulse. In this group, Professor Irving Babbitt of Harvard, Paul Elmer More, and the late Professor Stuart Sherman have been noteworthy figures. The following excerpts from their pens and the pens of others indicate something of their point of view, and of that of the opposition. The discussion is of great importance in any attempted appraisal of the tendencies in human conduct in our day.

THE HUMANIST [3]

By Irving Babbitt

disagrees with Rousseau.

Irving Babbitt is professor of French literature at Harvard University and the author of important works in the field of criticism. His name has come to be associated perhaps more than any other with the "new humanism." The excerpt which follows is from his book, *Literature and the American College.*

The humanist is equally on his guard against the excess of sympathy and the excess of selection, against the excess of liberty and the excess of restraint; he would have a restrained liberty and a sympathetic selection. He believes that the man of today, if he does not, like the man of the past, take on the yoke of a definite doctrine and discipline, must at least do inner obeisance to something higher than his ordinary self, whether he calls this something God, or, like the man of the Far East, calls it his higher Self, or simply the Law. Without this inner principle of restraint man can only oscillate

[3] Reprinted with the permission of the author and the publishers, Houghton Mifflin Company.

Humanist, believes in older standards of living.

violently between opposite extremes, like Rousseau, who said that for him there was "no intermediary term between everything and nothing." With this true restraint, on the other hand, he can harmonize these extremes and occupy the space between them. Rousseau, who would admit of no check upon the unruly desires of the heart (*libido sentiendi*), was therefore led to set up sympathy for one's fellow man as a substitute for religious obligation; and he combined this with a fierce assertion of man's rights and liberties. In encouraging men thus to put a sense of their rights above their obligations, he assumes that the unbounded self-assertion that results will have a sufficient offset in unbounded brotherhood. But is it true that the principle of sympathy will prevail, unaided, against the elemental forces of self-interest that Rousseau would unchain? Yes, replies the political economist, it will prevail if it has to deal with a self-interest that is properly enlightened. Unfortunately this whole search of our humanitarians for some ingenious mixture of altruistic sympathy and "enlightened self-interest" that will take the place of religious restraint, is too much of an order with the search on the physical plane for the secret of perpetual motion. . . .

Justice Brewer is reported to have said in a recent address that if the law of love only prevailed in the business world there would be no need of jails, no defaulting bank-cashiers, no over-reaching by individuals and trusts, etc. This is not thinking, but humanitarian reverie. If the world of business is ever governed by any law besides that of the wolf pack, it will not be by the law of love, but by the Ten Commandments, notably the commandment, Thou shalt not steal.

THE "INNER CHECK" [4]

By Stuart Sherman

This last phrase, "that she made lust and law alike in her decree, to take away the blame she had incurred," sums up for me a deep, many-branched ruinous tendency of contemporary thought. This is the logical conclusion of the naturalistic philosophy which has been for many years subtly extending its influence in all countries and in every field of human activity. It is the logical conclusion of repudiating all standards, teaching one's conscience to trot in the rut of events, and making one's truth as one needs it. The primitive savage is taught to believe that his happiness depends upon the observance of tabus. The modern savage is taught by a thousand sophists to believe that tabus are the only obstacles between him and his happiness. He "blasphemes the divine power" by identifying its dictates with his appetites, so that no check of religious superstition or of reasoned reverence remains in his consciousness to oppose the indefinite expansion of his "self-love." The devil, as Goethe represents him, is the spirit that denies. Mr. Paul Elmer More, certainly one of the most penetrating moralists of our times, says that this is

[4] Reprinted from The Introduction to On Contemporary Literature, with the permission of the publishers, Henry Holt and Company.

clean kam. The spirit that denies, he declares, is God. I
do not recall any single utterance from living lips that
has impressed me as more profoundly illuminating. I
should not like to think that denial is the only aspect of
God, but I am sure that is the aspect of God most ignored by those who flatter themselves that because they
have forgotten him he has forgotten them. And I am as
certain as I can be of anything that God is a spirit who
denies the validity of adopting the laws of the physical
universe for the moral regimen of man.

The great revolutionary task of nineteenth-century
thinkers, to speak it briefly, was to put man into nature.
The great task of twentieth-century thinkers is to get
him out again—somehow to break the spell of those
magically seductive cries, "Follow Nature," "Trust
your instincts," "Back to Nature." We have trusted our
instincts long enough to sound the depths of their
treacherousness. We have followed nature to the last
ditch and ditch water. . . .

In the natural world he [the humanist] discerns no
genuine law of progress, no conservation of values,
no unity of purpose, but brutal cross purposes, blind
chance, and everlasting change. The notion that the
Darwinian "survival of the fittest" indicates an aristocratic tendency in nature, he deems a vulgar error based
upon a confusion of adaptation to environment with
conformity to ideal ends. In human society, on the other
hand, Mr. Ibsen, for example, detects an "impetus,"
unique in character, which "urges us to bring our ex-
istences and the conditions about us into agreement with

an ideal picture we bear in our hearts." In the human consciousness Mr. More detects an "inner check" which, in the interest of character, opposes the push of instinct, the expansive impulse of the *élan vital.* "All the experience of the past," says Professor Babbitt, "cries, as though with a thousand tongues, through the manifold creeds and systems in which it has been very imperfectly formulated, that the highest human law is the law of concentration." To call this unique "impetus," this "inner check," this "law of concentration" human or to call it divine—is not this in the present state of our ideas a tolerably insignificant matter of nomenclature? Certainly the matter of quintessential importance is to recognize this impulse and to exalt it. For it cleaves the universe in twain as decisively as the fiat that divided the waters which were under the firmament from the waters which were above the firmament.

The line of progress for human society must therefore be in the direction of this human impetus. It cannot possibly lead "back to nature," but must steadily show a wider divergence from the path of natural evolution. Society is in great part an organized opposition to nature, and it justifies itself only when it maintains its ground. It is irrelevant to approve or condemn this or that possible line of conduct on the basis that it is or is not in conformity with nature. It is pertinent only to inquire whether it is in harmony with the constitution and aim of the human organization. It is not according to the tendency of clay to become a pot or of wood to become a table, but it is of the very essence of the artisan and the artist to overcome the tendency of wood and clay. It is according to the nature of an animal to preserve its own life and to reproduce its species, but it is of the essence of a man to lay down his life out of reverence for his great-grandfather and to check the impulse to indiscriminate reproduction out of consideration for his great-grandson. The impulse to refrain thus indicated we can find nowhere in nature. It is part of the pattern or design of human society that lies in the heart of man.

THE CRITICAL SPIRIT OF THE PURITAN TRADITION [5]

By Stuart Sherman

What have I been trying to demonstrate by this long review of the Puritan tradition? This, above all: that the Puritan is profoundly in sympathy with the modern spirit, is indeed the formative force in the modern spirit.

In order to make this point perfectly clear, I must take the liberty of repeating here what I have already said elsewhere by way of a description of the modern spirit:

"A great part of our lives, as we all feel in our educational period, is occupied with learning how to do and to be what others have been and have done before us. But presently we discover that the world is changing

[5] Reprinted from the essay, "What Is a Puritan?" in the volume, *The Genius of America*, with the permission of the publishers, Charles Scribner's Sons.

around us, and that the secrets of the masters and the experience of our elders do not wholly suffice to establish us effectively in our younger world. We discover within us needs, aspirations, powers, of which the generation that educated us seems unaware, or toward which it appears to be indifferent, unsympathetic, or even actively hostile. We perceive gradually or with successive shocks of surprise that many things which our fathers declared were true and satisfactory are not at all satisfactory, are by no means true, for us. Then it dawns upon us, perhaps as an exhilarating opportunity, perhaps as a grave and sobering responsibility, that in a little while we ourselves shall be the elders, the responsible generation. Our salvation in the day when we take command will depend, we believe, upon disentanglement from the lumber of heirlooms and hereditary devices, and upon the free, wise use of our own faculties."

At that moment, if we have inherited, not the Puritan heirlooms, but the living Puritan tradition, we enter into the modern spirit. By this phrase I mean, primarily, "the disposition to accept nothing on authority, but to bring all reports to the test of experience. The modern spirit is, first of all, a free spirit open on all sides to the influx of truth, *even from the past*. But freedom is not its only characteristic. The modern spirit is marked, further, by an active curiosity, which grows by what it feeds upon, and goes ever inquiring for fresher and sounder information, not content till it has the best information to be had anywhere. But since it seeks the best, it is, by necessity, also a critical spirit, constantly sifting, discriminating, rejecting, and holding fast that which is good, only till that which is better is within sight. This endless quest, when it becomes central in a life, requires labor, requires pain, requires a measure of courage; and so the modern spirit, with its other virtues, is an heroic spirit. As a reward for difficulties gallantly undertaken, the gods bestow on the modern spirit a kind of eternal youth, with unfailing powers of recuperation and growth."

To enter into this spirit is what the Puritan means by freedom. "He does not, like the false emancipator, merely cut us loose from the old moorings and set us adrift at the mercy of wind and tide. He comes aboard, like a good pilot; and while we trim our sails, he takes the wheel and lays our course for a fresh voyage. His message when he leaves us is not, 'Henceforth be masterless,' but 'Bear thou henceforth the scepter of thine own control through life and the passion of life.' " If that message still stirs us as with the sound of a trumpet, and frees and prepares us, not for the junketing of a purposeless vagabondage, but for the ardor and discipline and renunciation of a pilgrimage, we are Puritans.

FALSE GODS [6]

By Amy Loveman

The following paragraphs are taken from an editorial in *The Literary Review* of *The New York Evening Post,* August

[6] Reprinted with the permission of the author and of *The Literary Review* of the *New York Evening Post.*

18, 1923. Miss Loveman is at present associate editor of *The Saturday Review of Literature.*

charms *text,* *watchword'*

Every century has evolved its own shibboleth and fetiches and has thenceforth had to work its way to salvation through meshes of its own contriving. Our own age was prolific of them during the war years and is even now wrestling with the tangle which they precipitated. One of them was the doctrine of self-determination, which, translated from the sphere of international politics to the domain of literature, has meant the attaching of signal importance to self-expression as such. Another was the exaltation of speed and the corollary emphasis on production, which, again transferred to the realm of writing, finds its counterpart in the rapidity and mass of the literary output. Neither of these developments is of itself cause for congratulation; nay, rather are they both cause for serious concern. For the doctrine of self-expression has served as an excuse for a sudden outpouring of what an English schoolgirl, with a candor that some of our brash critics would do well to ponder, has inelegantly but expressively termed "mental slops," and the complacent acquiescence in the excellence of speed has borne fruit in an enormous mass of unseasoned writing.

Self-expression in the highest meaning of the term is indisputably a good. Indeed, it is almost axiomatic that no really great work can be produced that is not a direct outgrowth of the experience and mind that evolve it. All else is but pale imitation, the husk without the kernel, the shadow without the substance. That writer who is not expressing his own emotions and reactions but is drawing upon the feelings and attitudes of mind of others for his material must forever fail of the heights. But the mere fact that a writer to achieve truly meritorious work must express himself, in no way involves the deduction that because he is expressing himself his work must have value. Yet so some of our present-day critics would seem to wish us to believe. In their eyes self-revelation's the thing, and the disclosure of no matter what paltry philosophies, illicit desires, and undisciplined passions, is worthy of a respectful hearing merely because it is a record of self. We submit that any such contention as this is the veriest bunk—that there are purlieus of the mind and soul that no manner of literary skill in presenting them can ever render other than waste lands; that self-expression that translates into words experience either so commonplace or so intimate as to deserve the tribute of reticence is merely egotism run riot, and that criticism that fails to grade its interest by the caliber of the soul that is expressing itself is criticism not worth its salt. Oh, self-expression! What sins are committed in thy name! . . .

Part and parcel of the growing tendency to indiscriminate self-expression is the speed with which in these days we rush into print. No longer is bitter travail the prerequisite of literary birth. Everybody writes, and no sooner writes than seeks a publisher. And no sooner publishes than starts to write anew. Only the artist allows his soul to lie fallow, until in the fullness of time observation and feeling have enriched it for yielding;

and artists unfortunately are few among us. The rest, caught in the vortex of prevalent ideas, make a god of production and begin the first chapter of a new volume as they write finis to an old. Small wonder that all is grist that comes to their mill, whether it be the incidents of the life about them or the convulsions of their own souls. Perhaps it is unreasonable to quarrel with them that they should haste to print, for writers are men who must live by the proceeds of their labor and only the millionaire or the idealist can afford to write for posterity. It is a lonely business, starving for fame. Yet it is none the less deplorable for letters that the great god Production rules its estate and that in the confusion of values that results, anything can claim attention as literature provided it breaks new ground. We yield to experiment the same homage we give to self-expression; merely because it is experiment, no matter how extravagant, how half-baked, to a certain school it is thereby deserving of serious consideration. Had we less writing we should have more standards, and had we more standards we should have less leniency. Faith, hope, and charity, these are among the attributes that the critic of literature must possess, and the greatest of these is not always charity.

CRITICISM [7]

By Paul Elmer More

Paul Elmer More, scholar, author, and editor, is one of our ablest critics in the fields of thought and letters. His valua-

[7] Reprinted with the permission of the publishers, the Houghton Mifflin Company.

tions are based upon sound learning and careful weighing of evidence. The following quotation is from the essay "Criticism" in the Seventh Series of his *Shelburne Essays*.

There is, I trust, something more than a pedantic curiosity in such a parallel, which might yet be much prolonged, between the author of *Culture and Anarchy* and the author of the *Characteristics*.[8] It proves, if proof be necessary, more clearly than would any amount of direct exposition, that Matthew Arnold's method of criticism was not an isolated product of the nineteenth century, but that he belongs to one of the great families of human intelligence, which begins with Cicero, the father of them all, and passes through Erasmus and Boileau and Shaftesbury and Sainte-Beuve. These are the exemplars—not complete individually, I need not say—of what may be called the critical spirit: discriminators between the false and the true, the deformed and the normal; preachers of harmony and proportion and order, prophets of the religion of taste. If they deal much with the criticism of literature, this is because in literature more manifestly than anywhere else life displays its infinitely varied motives and results; and their practice is always to render literature itself more consciously a criticism of life. The past is the field out of which they draw their examples of what is in conformity with nature and of what departs from that norm. In that field they balance and weigh and measure; they are by intellect hesitators, but at heart very much in earnest. They are sometimes contrasted to their detri-

[8] Matthew Arnold and Anthony, Earl of Shaftesbury.

ment with the so-called creative writers, yet they themselves stood each among the first writers of his day, and
it is not plain that, for instance, Tennyson, in any true
estimation, added more to the intellectual life of the
world than Matthew Arnold, or Lucretius than Cicero,
though their method and aim may have been different.
The more significant comparison at least is not with
the so-called creative writers, but with the great ful-
minators of new creeds—between Matthew Arnold and
the Carlyles and Ruskins and Huxleys of his day; between Shaftesbury and, let us say, Rousseau; Boileau
and Descartes; Erasmus and Luther; Cicero and St. Paul.
Such a contrast might seem at first to lie as much in
efficiency as in quality. In the very nature of things the
man who seizes on one deep-reaching idea, whether
newly found or re-discovered, and with single-hearted
fervor forces it upon the world, might appear to have
the advantage in power over the man of critical temper,
who weighs and refines; who is forever checking the
enthusiasm of the living by the authority of the dead;
and whose doctrine, even though in the end he may
assert it with sovereign contempt of doubters, is still
the command to follow the well-tried path of common
sense. Better the half-truth that makes for action and
jostles the world out of its ruts, men cry, than such a
timid search for the whole truth as paralyzes the will,
and may after all prove only an exchange of depth for
breadth. That might appear to be the plain lesson of
history; yet I am not so sure. Is there not a possibility
that in our estimate of these powers we are a little be-

trayed by the tumult of the times, just as we are prone in other things to mistake bustle for movement? The critical spirit, as it has been exercised, may have its limitations and may justly be open to censure, but I doubt if its true reproach will turn out in the end to be a lack of efficiency in comparison with the more assertive force of the reformers. I am inclined to believe, for instance, that the balancing spirit of Erasmus is really more at work among us today than that of the dogmatic and reforming Luther; that Cicero's philosophy, though they would gape to hear it said, is really more in the hearts of the men you will meet in the street than is the theology of St. Paul. This may be in part because the representatives of the critical spirit, by their very lack of warping originality and by their endeavor to separate the true from the false, the complete from the one-sided, stand with the great conservative forces of human nature, having their fame certified by the things that endure amid all the betrayals of time and fashion.

THE FUNCTION OF THE CRITIC [9]

By J. E. Spingarn

Professor Spingarn, formerly a teacher of comparative literature at Columbia University, is one of the most brilliant of the American critics today. The following quotation is a part of his essay, "Scholarship and Criticism," which appears in *Civilization in the United States,* by Thirty Americans. The text is in the form revised by the author for a collection of essays, *Criticism in America: Its Function and Status.*

[9] Reprinted with the permission of Harcourt, Brace and Company.

When I wrote the essays which a few years later were collected in a volume bearing the subtitle of "Essays on the Unity of Genius and Taste," the pedants and the professors were in the ascendant, and it seemed necessary to emphasize the side of criticism which was then in danger, the side that is closest to the art of the creator. How unimportant it seemed then to weigh and define all the phases of a critic's duty, when one of the highest moments of the life of the spirit, the moment of artistic creation, appeared, at least in America, to be so completely misunderstood. But now the professors have been temporarily routed by the dilettanti, the amateurs, and the journalists, who treat a work of the imagination as if they were describing fireworks or a bull-fight (to use a phrase of Zola's about Gautier); and so it is necessary now to insist on the discipline and illumination of knowledge and thought—in other words, to write an "Essay on the Divergence of Criticism and Creation."

American criticism, like that of England, but to an even greater extent, suffers from a want of philosophic insight and precision. It has neither inherited nor created a tradition of esthetic thought. . . .

As a result, critics are constantly carrying on a guerilla warfare of their own in favor of some vague literary shibboleth or sociological abstraction, and discovering anew the virtues or vices of individuality, modernity, Puritanism, the romantic spirit or the spirit of the Middle West, the traditions of the pioneer, and so on ad infinitum. This holds true of every school of American criticism, "conservative" or "radical"; for all of them a disconnected body of literary theories takes the place of a real philosophy of art. "Find an idea and then write about it" sums up the average American writer's conception of criticism. There are even those who conceive this scattering of casual thoughts as the sole duty of a critic, on the extraordinary assumption that in this dispersion of thought and power the critic is "expressing himself" as an "artist." Now, while the critic must approach a work of literature without preconceived notion of what that individual work should attempt, he cannot criticize it without some understanding of what all literature attempts. The critic without an esthetic is a mariner without chart, compass, or knowledge of navigation; for the question is not where the ship should go or what cargo it should carry, but whether it is going to arrive at any port at all without sinking.

Criticism is essentially an expression of taste, or that faculty of imaginative sympathy by which the reader or spectator is able to relive the vision created by the artist. This is the soil without which it cannot flourish; but it attains its end and becomes criticism in the highest sense only when taste is guided by knowledge and rises to the level of thought, for then, and only then, does the critic give us something that the artist as artist cannot give. Of these three elements, implicit in all real criticism, the professors have made light of taste, and have made thought itself subservient to knowledge, while the dilettanti have considered it possible to dispense with both knowledge and thought. But even dilettante criticism is preferable to the dogmatic and intellectualist criticism of the professors, on the same grounds that Sainte-Beuve is superior to Brunetière, or Hazlitt to Francis Jeffrey; for the dilettante at least meets the mind of the artist on the plane of imagination and taste, while the intellectualist or moralist is precluded by his temperament and his theories from ever understanding the primal thrill and purpose of the creative act.

Back of any philosophy of art there must be a philosophy of life, and all esthetic formulae seem empty unless there is richness of content behind them. The critic, like the poet or the philosopher, has the whole world to range in, and the farther he ranges in it, the better his work will be. Yet this does not mean that criticism, in so far as it remains criticism of the arts of expression, should focus its attention on morals, history, life, instead of on the forms into which the artist transforms them. Art has something else to give us; and to seek moral or economic theories in it is to seek moral or economic theories, but not art. Indeed, the United States is the only civilized country where morals are still in controversy so far as creative literature is concerned; France, Germany, and Italy liberated themselves from this faded obsession long ago; even in England critics of authority hesitate to judge a work of art by moral standards. Yet this is precisely what divides the two chief schools of American criticism, the moralists and the anti-moralists, though even among the latter masquerade some whose only quarrel with the moralists is the nature of the moral standards employed.

The seeds of a more fruitful tradition had been planted in our earlier criticism, as we have seen. But if we disregard the influence of the "new psychology" and of a half-baked "literary anthropology," which has not yet taken definite form, the main forces that have influenced the present clashes in the American attitude toward literature seem to be three. There is first of all the conception of literature as a moral influence, a conception which goes back to the Græco-Roman rhetoricians and moralists, and after pervading English thought from Sidney to Johnson, finds its last stronghold today among the American descendants of the Puritans. There is, secondly, the Shavian conception of literature as the most effective instrument for the conversion of the world to a new *Weltanschauung*, to be judged by the novelty and freshness of its ideas, a conception particularly attractive to the school of young reformers, radicals, and intellectuals whose interest in the creative imagination is secondary, and whose training in esthetic thought has been negligible; this is merely an obverse of the Puritan moralism, and is tainted by the same fundamental misconception of the meaning of the creative imagination. And there is finally the conception of literature as an external thing, a complex of rhythms, charm, technical skill, beauty without inner content, or mere theatrical effectiveness, which goes back through the English nineties to the French seventies, when the idea of the spiritual autonomy of art—that "beauty is its own excuse for being"—was distorted into the merely mechanical theory of "art for art's sake"; the French have a special talent for narrowing esthetic truths into hard-and-fast formulae, devoid of their original nucleus of philosophic reality, but all the more effective on this account for universal conquest as practical programs. . . .

These are some of the elementary reasons why those who demand of the poet a definite code of morals or manners, the ready-made standards of any society, however great, that is bounded by space or time—"American ideals," or "Puritanism," or on the other side, "radical ideas"—seem to me to show their incompetence as critics. Life, teeming life, with all its ardors and agonies, is the only limit within which the poet's vision can be cabined and confined; and all we ask of him is that he create a new life in which the imagination can breathe and move as naturally as our practical selves can live in the world of reality. How can we expect illumination from those who share the "typical American business man's" inherent inability to live in the world of fantasy which the poets have created, without the business man's ability to face the external facts of life and mold them to his will? These men are schoolmasters, pedants, moralists, policemen, but neither critics nor true lovers of the spiritual food that art provides. To the creative writers of America I should give a wholly different message from theirs. I should say to them: "Express what is in you, all that serene or turbulent vision of multitudinous life which is yours by right of imagina-

tion, trusting in your own power to achieve discipline
and mastery, and leave the discussion of 'American
ideals' to statesmen, historians, and philosophers, with
the certainty that if you truly express the vision that is
in you, the statesmen, historians, and philosophers of the
future will point to your work as a fine expression of the
'American ideals' you have helped to create. Do not wait
for the flux of time to create a society that you can copy,
but create your own society; and if you are a great
writer it will be a Great Society, which the world will
never cease to live in and to love. For you America
must always be not old but new, something unrealized,
something to be created and to be given as an incredible
gift to a hundred million men. Courage is the birth-
right of the poet as much as of the soldier or statesman;
and courage in trusting your imagination is to you the
very breath of life. But mastery of the imagination, and
not mere submission to it, must be your goal; for how
can the true artist express himself in terms of slavery
rather than power? By giving what is best in him to his
art, the American artist serves America best."

A profound inner reform is needed in order that the
critics of America may prepare themselves adequately to
interpret this new literature, to separate the chaff from
the wheat, and in so doing to purify and ennoble the
taste and enlarge the imaginative sympathies of a whole
people.

The first need of American criticism today is education in esthetic thinking. It needs above all the cleansing
and stimulating power of an intellectual bath. Only the

drenching discipline that comes from mastery of the problems of esthetic thought can train us for the duty of interpreting the American literature of the future. The anarchy of impressionism is a natural reaction against the mechanical theories and jejune text-books of the professors, but it is a temporary haven and not a home. The haphazard empiricism of English criticism and the faded moralism of some of our own will serve us no more. We must desert these muddy waters, and seek purer and deeper streams. For the conception of the critic as megaphone or phonograph we must substitute the conception of the critic as esthetic thinker. In a country where philosophers urge men to cease thinking, it may be the task of the critic to revivify and reorganize thought.

The second need of American criticism can be summed up in the word scholarship—that discipline of knowledge which will give us at one and the same time a wider international outlook and a deeper national insight. One will spring from the other, for the timid Colonial spirit finds no place in the heart of the citizen of the world; and respect for native talent, born of a surer knowledge, will prevent us alike from overrating its merits and from holding it too cheap. For the lifeless pedantry of the professors, who think that tradition actually lives in monuments, heirlooms, dead ancestors, and printed books, we must substitute the illumination of a humane scholarship, which realizes that learning is but a quest for the larger self and that tradition is a state of the soul. Half-knowledge is either too timid or too cocksure; and only out of the spiritual discipline that is born of intellectual travail and adventure can come a true independence of judgment and taste.

For taste is after all both the point of departure and the goal; and the third and greatest need of American criticism is a deeper sensibility, a more complete submission to the imaginative will of the artist, before attempting to rise above it into the realm of judgment. The critic is not a man seated on a block of ice watching a bright fire, or how could he realize the full force of its warmth and power? If there is anything that American life can be said to give least of all, it is training in taste. There is a deadness of artistic feeling, which is sometimes replaced or disguised by a fervor of sociological obsession, but this is no substitute for the faculty of imaginative sympathy which is at the heart of all criticism. By taste, I mean, of course, not the "good taste" of the dilettante or the amateur collector, or taste in its eighteenth-century sense, but that creative moment of the life of the spirit which the artist and the enjoyer of art share alike. For this the ardor of the reformer, the insight of the historian, even the moral passion of the saint is no substitute; for taste, or esthetic enjoyment, is the only gateway to the critic's judgment, and over it is a flaming signpost, "Critic, abandon all hope when this gate is shut."

This is your task, critics of America—to see that Plato's dream of banishing poets from the ideal Republic does not come true. It is your chief duty, against moralist and hedonist and utilitarian alike, to justify the ways of beauty to Americans. In a land where virtuous platitudes have so often been mistaken for poetry, it is your task to explain the real meaning of the esthetic moment for the higher lives of men. But no one knows better than I that you cannot rest satisfied even with this. For the modern critic has learnt to distinguish clearly between art, philosophy, history, religion, morals, not for the purpose of denying but of establishing their essential unity in the life of the spirit. Those who deny this unity and those who would substitute for it a muddle-headed if well-meaning confusion are alike the Enemy. Though you reject the criticism in which beauty is forever measured and tested by the moralist's rigid rules and justified by virtues that are not her own, still less can you be satisfied with the criticism in which "ideas" are struck out in random and irresponsible flashes like sparks from the anvil of a gnome. You cannot be satisfied with anything but truth—that whole truth which is life—even in the service of beauty.

DISCUSSION AND THEME TOPICS

1. What do you think would be the result if you should decide to set up impulse and desire as the sole guides of your daily conduct, without the checks which reason and judgment provide? Suppose, too, that every one about you should do the same thing. Poets and philosophers have dreamed of Utopias and golden ages, of Edens before sin entered, of islands of the South Seas where life was unsullied by civilization. How far would you trust such conditions for the making possible of an ideal so-

ciety? See if you can make a thoughtful evaluation of Rousseau's demand for a "return to nature."

2. As you watch the great majority of the people about you in the daily routine of their lives, their mental activities, their reading, their amusements, their social contacts, their churches, their clubs, the thousand things which fill the days of their allotted three-score years and ten, would you say that they are guided chiefly by the Hebraic, Hellenistic, or Rousseauistic spirit, as you understand the essential meaning of each of these? Is their conduct governed by obedience to law (which they may believe divine), or by enlightened intelligence, or by impulse and desire? Or perhaps you find all of these factors operative in the lives of most people. What groups are pretty good illustrations of the predominant control of one or the other of these forces? In what groups do you find the highest wisdom for guidance in matters of civic and national concern, for the maintenance of individual and public honor, or for expression in literature and the arts?

3. How are you impressed by Emerson's essay, "Self-Reliance," from which an excerpt is given in this chapter? Read it in its complete form. Is Emerson right about the worth of individuality? But suppose that every member of the race which Mencken calls *homo boobiens* should set himself up as a god and demand the right both to be and to be heard. What glory lies in the assertion and expression of the lackwit or rascal? Does Emerson overstate the case at any point? Is the convincing power of the essay thereby lost? One vigorous thinker has called the teaching of the essay "pure Rousseauism." Is it?

4. Select a group of perhaps three moving pictures that are widely popular and try to analyze the secret of their appeal to the public. Does the popularity of such films constitute damaging evidence regarding the quality of our civilization? Discuss the matter pro and con, and present your own ideas.

5. Make a similar analysis of one or more plays of this season

or last which were undoubted Broadway successes. Should
we look back with envious and longing eyes to the golden
days of Greek drama, and admit with shame the decadence of our times?

6. Do the magazines which sell most widely on the news
stands pay tribute to the taste and intelligence of contemporary America? It might be interesting to examine
the contents of two or three of the best sellers among the
periodicals and to see what the study reveals.

7. Perhaps you resent the readiness with which certain
critics charge the masses of mankind with cheapness,
ignorance, and vulgarity. Mr. Mencken is an admirable
one to center your attack upon in a theme. But do not
attempt to compete with him in vituperative style. Write
sincerely in your own way.

8. Read "Wanted: A Substitute for Righteousness" by Avis
D. Carlson in *Harper's Magazine*, January, 1927, and
write down your impression of her novel suggestion.

9. Read Stuart Sherman's chapter, "The Barbaric Naturalism of Dreiser," in the book *On Contemporary Literature*,
and write a discussion of his criticism of the unrestrained
working of impulse in Theodore Dreiser's novels.

10. Write a statement of what you regard as the function of
the critic in the field of literature today. If he attains to
the highest service of which criticism is capable, what is
the nature of that service? What is his relation to the
creative genius? Do you expect from him a statement
of personal opinion, or a record of the emotions of a
sensitive soul detailing his "adventures among master-
pieces," or a judicial appraisal based upon accepted canons
of taste?

11. What do you regard as the requirements of the critic, the
qualities of mind and of nature which he must bring to
his task if his judgments are to have weight? What mental traits or critical methods, on the other hand, lead to a
discrediting of his views? Write a discussion of the whole
question based upon principles presented in the text.
This theme could readily be expanded into a treatise of
some length.

SUGGESTIONS FOR MORE EXTENDED STUDY

1. Make a study of Rousseau's exaltation of the natural man. Read *La nouvelle Héloïse* and *Emile* and make an analysis of his defense of impulse and emotion as opposed to intellect and custom.

2. Read such essays of Matthew Arnold as "Sweetness and Light," "Hebraism and Hellenism," and "The Function of Criticism," and analyze what you regard as the essential quality of his approach to life.

3. Read somewhat widely in H. L. Mencken's writings, particularly in the "Prejudices" (entire series), and see if you can arrive at an understanding of his point of view. Present this critically, and include a discussion of the style or manner in which he sets it forth.

4. Read in a similar fashion among the books of Stuart Sherman, such as *On Contemporary Literature, Americans, The Genius of America,* and *Critical Woodcuts,* and analyze critically his literary faith. Do you find that this changes at all between the first and the last of the above-mentioned books?

5. Read and discuss critically any one of the following:
    a. *Civilization in the United States,* by Thirty Americans.
    b. A group of Emerson's essays which set forth his approach to the conduct of life.
    c. A group of Whitman's poems and the philosophy of life which you find implicit in them.
    d. Representative essays of Paul Elmer More.

VOCABULARY LIST

hedonist	affinity *to complet*	quintessential	Shavian
ramifications	complementary	latent	nomenclature
myriad	ineffaceable	disseminate	shibboleth *slogan*
admonition	ephemeral	obviously	fetish
sordid	lintels	indomitable	purlieu
paramount	oscillate	felicity	reticence

indiscriminate	*Weltanschauung*	crass	altruistic
Messianic	idiosyncrasy	multiform	humanitarian
catalytic	ineffable	acquiescence	tabus
catharsis	superincumbent	epistemological	repudiating
ingratiating	megalomania	immutable	chagrined
cosmic	inhibition	tenacity	patriarch
fulminator	ethical	alienated	ingenious
capitulate	dilettanti	absolve	*élan vital*
autonomy	jejune	affectation	exhilarating
laudable	empiricism	appraisal	prolific
glibly	syllogism	offset	travail

READING LIST

The list comprises the sources from which the selections in the text are taken, and other works bearing upon the discussion of the chapter.

Lane Cooper. *Two Views of Education*. New Haven, 1922.

Will Durant. *The Story of Philosophy*. New York, 1926.

Matthew Arnold. "Hebraism and Hellenism," in *Culture and Anarchy*.

Ralph Waldo Emerson. *Essays*.

Irving Babbitt. *Literature and the American College*. Boston, 1908.

——*Rousseau and Romanticism*. Boston, 1919.

——"Genius and Taste," in *The Nation*, February 7, 1918.

Stuart Sherman. *On Contemporary Literature*. New York, 1917.

——*Americans*. New York, 1922.

——*The Genius of America*. New York, 1923.

——*Critical Woodcuts*. New York, 1926.

Amy Loveman. Editorial, "False Gods," in *Literary Review* (*New York Evening Post*), August 18, 1922.

Paul Elmer More. *Shelburne Essays*. Boston. Seventh Series, 1910. Ninth Series, *Aristocracy and Justice*, 1915.

J. E. Spingarn. "Scholarship and Criticism," in *Civilization in the United States*. New York, 1922.

——*Creative Criticism: Essays on the Unity of Genius and Taste.* New York, 1917.

Ludwig Lewisohn. *A Modern Book of Criticisms.* New York, 1918.

H. L. Mencken. *Prejudices,* First, Second, Third, Fourth, Fifth and Sixth Series. New York, 1919-26.

——*Criticism in America: Its Function and Status.* New York, 1924.

George Santayana. *Little Essays.* New York, 1920.

Chapter IV

FREEDOM OF THOUGHT; LIBERTY OF THE INDIVIDUAL; THE RULE OF THE MAJORITY; DEMOCRACY

The conflict between the desire for self-expression on the one hand and the forces that limit and direct that expression on the other, becomes in society a clash between the personal freedom of the individual and the supposed welfare of the group of which he is a part. The curtailment of individual liberty beyond a low minimum of control has from time immemorial and almost universally been vigorously resented. In government, in religion, and in personal conduct, people have believed that they have an inalienable right to direct their own affairs. In our own age the "time-spirit" is marked by the note of revolt, repudiation of society controls, irritation at over-zealous legislation which invades the field of private conduct, and by the assertion of the right of the individual to "live his own life." In opposition to this spirit of independence, there are equally militant forces which seek through the machinery of government to mold the world nearer to their heart's desire. The extent to which control may legitimately be employed to secure the greatest good for all has long been a matter of controversy, and the problem obviously admits of no arbitrary settlement. Yet certain principles may be discovered to serve as a framework upon which to fashion our common life. There are many people who refuse to relinquish the belief that the human mind will eventually be able to work out a series of adjustments by which life can be lived successfully by men in this world. It was the hope of the nineteenth century that democracy, the rule of the majority, might, through popular enlightenment, come to be the rule of excellence, but in these latter years we are not so sure.

Various phases of the discussion are presented in the following pages.

ON THE LIBERTY OF THOUGHT AND DISCUSSION
By John Stuart Mill

There can hardly be any other point of departure in the discussion which is before us than the masterful essay on liberty by John Stuart Mill. As a piece of closely reasoned exposition, brilliant in form and matter, the essay is one of the high-water marks of intellectual attainment in the nineteenth century. Mill is here primarily concerned with freedom in the realm of thought and expression, but he builds his argument upon principles which he deems fundamental in the problem of human liberty as a whole. Our quotation is taken from the second chapter.

The time, it is to be hoped, is gone by, when any defense would be necessary of the "liberty of the press" as one of the securities against corrupt or tyrannical government. No argument, we may suppose, can now be needed, against permitting a legislature or an executive, not identified in interest with the people, to prescribe opinions to them, and determine what doctrines or what arguments they shall be allowed to hear. This aspect of the question, besides, has been so often and so triumphantly enforced by preceding writers, that it need not be specially insisted on in this place. Though the law of England, on the subject of the press, is as servile to this day as it was in the time of the Tudors, there is little danger of its being actually put in force against political discussion, except during some temporary panic, when fear of insurrection drives ministers and judges from their propriety; and, speaking generally, it is not, in constitutional countries, to be apprehended that the government, whether completely responsible to the people or not, will often attempt to control the expression of opinion, except when in doing so it makes itself the organ of the general intolerance of the public. Let us suppose, therefore, that the government is entirely at one with the people, and never thinks of exerting any power of coercion unless in agreement with what it conceives to be their voice. But I deny the right of the people to exercise such coercion, either by themselves or by their government. The power itself is illegitimate. The best government has no more title to it than the worst. It is as noxious, or more noxious, when exerted in accordance with public opinion than when in opposition to it. If all mankind, minus one, were of one opinion, and only one person were of the contrary opinion, mankind would be no more justified in silencing that one person than he, if he had the power, would be justified in silencing mankind. Were an opinion a personal possession of no value except to the owner; if to be obstructed in the enjoyment of it were simply a private injury, it would make some difference whether the injury was inflicted only on a few persons or on many. But the peculiar evil of silencing the expression of an opinion is, that it is robbing the human race; posterity as well as the existing generation; those who dissent from the opinion, still more than those who hold it. If the opinion is right, they are deprived of the opportunity of exchanging error for truth; if wrong, they lose what is almost as great a benefit, the clearer perception and livelier impression of truth, produced by its collision with error.

It is necessary to consider separately these two hypotheses, each of which has a distinct branch of the argument corresponding to it. We can never be sure that the opinion we are endeavoring to stifle is a false opinion; and if we were sure, stifling it would be an evil still.

First: the opinion which it is attempted to suppress by authority may possibly be true. Those who desire to suppress it, of course, deny its truth; but they are not infallible. They have no authority to decide the question for all mankind, and exclude every other person from the means of judging. To refuse a hearing to an opinion, because they are sure that it is false, is to assume that *their* certainty is the same thing as *absolute* certainty. All silencing of discussion is an assumption of infallibility. Its condemnation may be allowed to rest on this common argument, not the worse for being common.

Unfortunately for the good sense of mankind, the fact of their fallibility is far from carrying the weight in their practical judgment which is always allowed to it in theory; for while every one well knows himself to be fallible, few think it necessary to take any precautions against their own fallibility, or admit the supposition that any opinion, of which they feel very certain, may be one of the examples of the error to which they acknowledge themselves to be liable. Absolute princes, or others who are accustomed to unlimited deference, usually feel this complete confidence in their own opinions on nearly all subjects. People more happily situated, who sometimes hear their opinions disputed, and are not wholly unused to be set right when they are wrong, place the same unbounded reliance only on such of their opinions as are shared by all who surround them, or to whom they habitually defer; for in proportion to a man's want of confidence in his own solitary judgment does he usually repose, with implicit trust, on the infallibility of "the world" in general. And the world, to each individual, means the part of it with which he comes in contact; his party, his sect, his church, his class of society: the man may be called, by comparison, almost liberal and large-minded to whom it means anything so comprehensive as his own country or his own age. Nor is his faith in this collective authority at all shaken by his being aware that other ages, countries, sects, churches, classes, and parties have thought, and even now think, the exact reverse. He devolves upon his own world the responsibility of being in the right

against the dissentient worlds of other people; and it
never troubles him that mere accident has decided which
of these numerous worlds is the object of his reliance,
and that the same causes which make him a Churchman
in London would have made him a Buddhist or a Confu-
cian in Pekin. Yet it is as evident in itself as any amount
of argument can make it, that ages are no more infallible than individuals; every age having held many opinions which subsequent ages have deemed not only false
but absurd; and it is as certain that many opinions, now
general, will be rejected by future ages, as it is that
many once general are rejected by the present.

The objection likely to be made to this argument
would probably take some such form as the following:
There is no greater assumption of infallibility in forbidding the propagation of error than in any other thing
which is done by public authority on its own judgment
and responsibility. Judgment is given to men that they
may use it. Because it may be used erroneously, are men
to be told that they ought not to use it at all? To
prohibit what they think pernicious is not claiming ex-
emption from error, but fulfilling the duty incumbent
on them, although fallible, of acting on their conscientious conviction. If we were never to act on our opinions, because those opinions may be wrong, we should
leave all our interests uncared for, and all our duties un-
performed. An objection which applies to all conduct
can be no valid objection to any conduct in particular.
It is the duty of governments, and of individuals, to
form the truest opinions they can; to form them care-

fully, and never impose them upon others unless they are quite sure of being right. But when they are sure (such reasoners may say), it is not conscientiousness but cowardice to shrink from acting on their opinions, and allow doctrines which they honestly think dangerous to the welfare of mankind, either in this life or in another, to be scattered abroad without restraint, because other people, in less enlightened times, have persecuted opinions now believed to be true. Let us take care, it may be said, not to make the same mistake; but governments and nations have made mistakes in other things, which are not denied to be fit subjects for the exercise of authority; they have laid on bad taxes, made unjust wars. Ought we therefore to lay on no taxes, and, under whatever provocation, make no wars? Men and governments must act to the best of their ability. There is no such thing as absolute certainty, but there is assurance sufficient for the purposes of human life. We may, and must, assume our opinion to be true for the guidance of our own conduct; and it is assuming no more when we forbid bad men to pervert society by the propagation of opinions which we regard as false and pernicious.

I answer that it is assuming very much more. There is the greatest difference between presuming an opinion to be true, because, with every opportunity for contesting it, it has not been refuted, and assuming its truth for the purpose of not permitting its refutation. Complete liberty of contradicting and disproving our opinion is the very condition which justifies us in assuming its truth for purposes of action; and on no other terms can a being with human faculties have any rational assurance of being right.

When we consider either the history of opinion, or the ordinary conduct of human life, to what is it to be ascribed that the one and the other are no worse than they are? Not, certainly, to the inherent force of the human understanding; for, on any matter not self-evident, there are ninety-nine persons totally incapable of judging of it, for one who is capable; and the capacity of the hundredth person is only comparative; for the majority of the eminent men of every past generation held many opinions now known to be erroneous, and did or approved numerous things which no one will now justify. Why is it, then, that there is on the whole a preponderance among mankind of rational opinions and rational conduct? If there really is this preponderance —which there must be, unless human affairs are, and have always been, in an almost desperate state—it is owing to a quality of the human mind, the source of everything respectable in man either as an intellectual or as a moral being; namely, that his errors are corrigible. He is capable of rectifying his mistakes, by discussion and experience. Not by experience alone. There must be discussion, to show how experience is to be interpreted. Wrong opinions and practices gradually yield to fact and argument; but facts and arguments, to produce any effect on the mind, must be brought before it. Very few facts are able to tell their own story, without comments to bring out their meaning. The whole strength and value, then, of human judgment, depending on the one property, that it can be set right when it is wrong, reliance can be placed on it only when the means of setting it right are kept constantly at hand. In the case of any person whose judgment is really deserving of confidence, how has it become so? Because he has kept his mind open to criticism of his opinions and conduct. Because it has been his practice to listen to all that could be said against him; to profit by as much of it as was just, and expound to himself, and upon occasion to others, the fallacy of what was fallacious. Because he has felt that the only way in which a human being can make some approach to knowing the whole of a subject is by hearing what can be said about it by persons of every variety of opinion, and studying all modes in which it can be looked at by every character of mind. No wise man ever acquired his wisdom in any mode but this; nor is it in the nature of human intellect to become wise in any other manner. The steady habit of correcting and completing his own opinion by collating it with those of others, so far from causing doubt and hesitation in carrying it into practice, is the only stable foundation for a just reliance on it; for, being cognizant of all that can, at least obviously, be said against him, and having taken up his position against all gainsayers— knowing that he has sought for objections and difficulties, instead of avoiding them, and has shut out no light which can be thrown upon the subject from any quarter—he has a right to think his judgment better than that of any person, or any multitude, who have not gone through a similar process. . . .

But, indeed, the dictum that truth always triumphs over persecution is one of those pleasant falsehoods which men repeat after one another till they pass into commonplaces, but which all experience refutes. History teems with instances of truth put down by persecution. If not suppressed forever, it may be thrown back for centuries. To speak only of religious opinions: the Reformation broke out at least twenty times before Luther, and was put down. Arnold of Brescia was put down. Fra Dolcino was put down. Savonarola was put down. The Albigeois were put down. The Vaudois were put down. The Lollards were put down. The Hussites were put down. Even after the era of Luther, wherever persecution was persisted in, it was successful. In Spain, Italy, Flanders, the Austrian empire, Protestantism was rooted out; and, most likely, would have been so in England, had Queen Mary lived, or Queen Elizabeth died. Persecution has always succeeded, save where the heretics were too strong a party to be effectually persecuted. No reasonable person can doubt that Christianity might have been extirpated in the Roman Empire. It spread and became predominant, because the persecutions were only occasional, lasting but a short time, and separated by long intervals of almost undisturbed propagandism. It is a piece of idle sentimentality that truth, merely as truth, has any inherent power denied to error, of prevailing against the dungeon and the stake. Men are not more zealous for truth than they often are for error, and a sufficient application of legal or even of social penalties will generally succeed in stopping the propagation of either. The real advantage which truth has consists in this: that when an opinion is true, it may be extinguished once, twice, or many times, but in the course of ages there will generally be found persons to rediscover it, until some one of its reappearances falls on a time when from favorable circumstances it escapes persecution until it has made such head as to withstand all subsequent attempts to suppress it. . . .

Those in whose eyes this reticence on the part of heretics is no evil should consider in the first place that in consequence of it there is never any fair and thorough discussion of heretical opinions; and that such of them as could not stand such a discussion, though they may be prevented from spreading, do not disappear. But it is not the minds of heretics that are deteriorated most by the ban placed on all inquiry which does not end in the orthodox conclusions. The greatest harm done is to those who are not heretics, and whose whole mental development is cramped, and their reason cowed, by the fear of heresy. Who can compute what the world loses in the multitude of promising intellects combined with timid characters, who dare not follow out any bold, vigorous, independent train of thought, lest it should land them in something which would admit of being considered irreligious or immoral? Among them we may occasionally see some man of deep conscientiousness, and subtle and refined understanding, who spends a life in sophisticating with an intellect which he cannot silence, and exhausts the resources of ingenuity in attempting to reconcile the promptings of his conscience and reason with orthodoxy, which yet he does not, perhaps, to the end succeed in doing. No one can be a great thinker who does not recognize that as a thinker it is his first duty to follow his intellect to whatever conclusions it may lead. Truth gains more even by the errors of one who, with due study and preparation, thinks for himself, than by the true opinions of those who only hold them because they do not suffer themselves to think. Not that it is solely, or chiefly, to form great thinkers, that freedom of thinking is required. On the contrary, it is as much, and even more indispensable, to enable average human beings to attain the mental stature which they are capable of. There have been, and may again be, great individual thinkers, in a general atmosphere of mental slavery. But there never has been, nor ever will be, in that atmosphere, an intellectually active people. Where any people has made a temporary approach to such a character, it has been because the dread of heterodox speculation was for a time suspended. Where there is a tacit convention that principles are not to be disputed; where the discussion of the greatest questions which can occupy humanity is considered to be closed, we cannot hope to find that generally high scale of mental activity which has made some periods of history so remarkable. Never when controversy avoided the subjects which are large and important enough to kindle enthusiasm was the mind of a people stirred up from its foundations, and the impulse given which raised even persons of the most ordinary intellect to something of the dignity of thinking beings. Of such we have had an example in the condition of Europe during the times immediately following the Reformation; another, though limited to the Continent and to a more cultivated class, in the speculative movement of the latter half of the eighteenth century; and a third, of still briefer duration, in the intellectual fermentation of Germany during the Goethean and Fichtean period. These periods differed widely in the particular opinions which they developed, but were alike in this, that during all three the yoke of authority was broken. In each, an old mental despotism had been thrown off, and no new one had yet taken its place. The impulse given at these three periods has made Europe what it now is. Every single improvement which has taken place either in the human mind or in institutions may be traced distinctly to one or other of them. Appearances have for some time indicated that all three impulses are well-nigh spent, and we can expect no fresh start until we again assert our mental freedom.

Let us now pass to the second division of the argument, and dismissing the supposition that any of the received opinions may be false, let us assume them to be true, and examine into the worth of the manner in which they are likely to be held, when their truth is not freely and openly canvassed. However unwillingly a person who has a strong opinion may admit the possibility that his opinion may be false, he ought to be moved by the consideration that however true it may be, if it is not fully, frequently, and fearlessly discussed, it will be held as a dead dogma, not a living truth.

There is a class of persons (happily not quite so numerous as formerly) who think it enough if a person assents undoubtingly to what they think true, though he has no knowledge whatever of the grounds of the opinion, and could not make a tenable defense of it against the most superficial objections. Such persons, if they can once get their creed taught from authority, naturally think that no good, and some harm, comes of its being allowed to be questioned. Where their influence prevails, they make it nearly impossible for the received opinion to be rejected wisely and considerately, though it may still be rejected rashly and ignorantly; for to shut out discussion entirely is seldom possible, and when it once gets in, beliefs not grounded on conviction are apt to give way before the slightest semblance of an argument. Waiving, however, this possibility—assuming that the true opinion abides in the mind, but abides as a prejudice, a belief independent of, and proof against, argument—this is not the way in which truth ought to be held by a rational being. This is not knowing the truth. Truth, thus held, is but one superstition the more, accidentally clinging to the words which enunciate a truth. . . .

But when we turn to subjects infinitely more complicated—to morals, religion, politics, social relations, and the business of life—three-fourths of the arguments for every disputed opinion consist in dispelling the appearances which favor some opinion different from it. The greatest orator, save one, of antiquity, has left it on record that he always studied his adversary's case with

as great, if not with still greater, intensity than even
his own. What Cicero practiced as the means of forensic *argumentation*
success, requires to be imitated by all who study any
subject in order to arrive at the truth. He who knows
only his own side of the case knows little of that. His
reasons may be good, and no one may have been able
to refute them. But if he is equally unable to refute the
reasons on the opposite side; if he does not so much as
know what they are, he has no ground for preferring
either opinion. The rational position for him would be
suspension of judgment, and unless he contents himself
with that, he is either led by authority, or adopts, like
the generality of the world, the side to which he feels
most inclination. Nor is it enough that he should hear
the arguments of adversaries from his own teachers,
presented as they state them, and accompanied by what
they offer as refutations. That is not the way to do justice to the arguments, or bring them into real contact
with his own mind. He must be able to hear them from
persons who actually believe them, who defend them in
earnest and do their very utmost for them. He must
know them in their most plausible and persuasive form;
he must feel the whole force of the difficulty which the
true view of the subject has to encounter and dispose
of; else he will never really possess himself of the portion of truth which meets and removes that difficulty.
Ninety-nine in a hundred of what are called educated
men are in this condition, even those who can argue
fluently for their opinions. Their conclusion may be
true, but it might be false for anything they know;

they have never thrown themselves into the mental position of those who think differently from them, and considered what such persons may have to say; and consequently they do not, in any proper sense of the word, know the doctrine which they themselves profess. They do not know those parts of it which explain and justify the remainder; the considerations which show that a fact which seemingly conflicts with another is reconcilable with it, or that of two apparently strong reasons, one and not the other ought to be preferred. All that part of the truth which turns the scale and decides the judgment of a completely informed mind, they are strangers to; nor is it ever really known, but to those who have attended equally and impartially to both sides, and endeavored to see the reasons of both in the strongest light. So essential is this discipline to a real understanding of moral and human subjects, that if opponents of all important truths do not exist, it is indispensable to imagine them, and supply them with the strongest arguments which the most skillful devil's advocate can conjure up.

THE ABRIDGMENT OF LIBERTY [1]

By James C. Carter

In a course of lectures which were prepared for delivery before the Harvard University Law School and which appeared eventually in his book, *Law: Its Origin, Growth, and Function*, James C. Carter indicates a basis on which he be-

[1] Reprinted with the permission of the publishers, G. P. Putnam's Sons.

lieves the liberty of the individual may be curtailed. The excerpt quoted is from Lecture XIII.

But the largest field for the employment of the conscious agency of society in the improvement of the law is to be found in the multiplied forms of legislation which a highly developed industrial life demands. When we consider the enormous mass of apparently necessary legislation found in modern societies, we are almost led to doubt the soundness of the maxim that the best government is that which governs least, as well as the soundness of the teaching that the sole function of government and of law is to secure to every man the largest possible freedom of individual action consistent with the preservation of the like liberty for every other man; but while these maxims are permanently and everywhere true, the actual amount of government control varies according to social conditions. In rural communities, with their sparse populations engaged almost entirely in agricultural pursuits, comparatively little legislative interference with the conduct of life is needed. A simple organization of the civil power under officers such as sheriffs and constables, a suitable provision of judicial tribunals for the determination of civil disputes and the punishment of crime, simple provisions for the maintenance of roads and bridges, schools, poor-houses, and jails are all that is necessary. But the division of employments attendant upon advancing civilization and the consequent increase of coöperation, and crowded populations in cities, towns, and villages, present very different conditions. Men touch each other in a vastly greater number of ways and may consequently the more encroach upon and abridge the individual liberty of each other. These encroachments, if left to the natural mode of redress, would involve continual strife. Moreover, such populations have many common additional needs to which all must contribute. Streets, pavements, sewers, light, police, must be provided for, and these require many laws and regulations. Banking, insurance, and other methods of business coöperation are demanded; but these would, through the fraud or neglect of those entrusted with the management, be perverted to the injury of the ignorant or unskillful, unless a system of government supervision were maintained. Additional and more complex legislation is therefore demanded as society advances, but the principles which should guide that legislation and determine its amount remain the same. Where is the line to be drawn beyond which compulsory laws should not be permitted to pass? What are the maxims which should reconcile liberty and restraint? There is no clearly perceivable line which enables us in every case to clearly determine how far society may go in limiting and directing individual conduct. It changes with the changing conditions of life. But there is a guide which, when kept clearly and constantly in view, sufficiently informs us what we should attempt to do by legislation and what should be left to other agencies. This is what I have so often insisted upon as the sole function both of law and legislation; namely, to secure to each individual the utmost liberty which he can enjoy consistently with the preservation of like liberty to all others. Liberty, the first of blessings, the aspiration of every human soul, is the supreme object. Every abridgment of it demands an excuse, and the only good excuse is the necessity of preserving it. Whatever tends to preserve this is right; all else is wrong. To leave each man to work out in freedom his own happiness or misery, to stand or fall by the consequences of his own conduct, is the true method of human discipline. For myself, I reject that view of the cosmic scheme which would regard society as the unit for the well-being of which our efforts should be immediately directed, even though individual happiness and perfection were thereby sacrificed. The society most perfect, as a whole, will be that alone which is composed of the most perfect and happy individuals.

INTOLERANCE IN DEMOCRACIES [2]

By James Bryce

James Bryce, eminent statesman and ambassador, in his book, *Modern Democracies,* asks for the recognition of the prophet of dissent in the discussions of popular government.

We perceive that the enthusiasm for liberty which fired men's hearts for a century or more from the beginning of the American Revolution down to our own time has now grown cool. The dithyrambic expression it found in the poets and orators of those days sounds strange and hollow in the ears of the present genera-

[2] Reprinted by permission of and arrangement with the publishers, the Macmillan Company. Copyright, 1921.

tion, bent on securing, with the least possible exertion, the material conditions of comfort and well-being.

Liberty may not have achieved all that was expected; yet it remains true that nothing was more vital to national progress than the spontaneous development of individual character, and that free play of intellect which is independent of current prejudice, examines everything in the light of reason and history, and fearlessly defends unpopular opinions. Independence of thought was formerly threatened by monarchs who feared the disaffection of their subjects. May it not again be threatened by other forms of intolerance, possible even in a popular government?

Room should be found in every country for men who, like the prophets in ancient Israel, have, along with their wrath at the evils of their own time, inspiring visions of a better future and the right to speak their minds. That love of freedom which will bear with opposition because it has faith in the victory of truth is none too common. Many of those who have the word on their lips are despots at heart. Those men in whom that love seemed to glow with the hottest flame may have had an almost excessive faith in its power for good, but if this be an infirmity, it is an infirmity of noble minds, which democracies ought to honor.

Not less than any other form of government does democracy need to cherish individual liberty. It is, like oxygen in the air, a life-giving spirit. Political liberty will have seen one of its fairest fruits wither on the bough if that spirit should decline.

THE LOSS OF LIBERTY FOR THE MINORITY [3]

By Arthur Twining Hadley

The quotation is from an article by Arthur Twining Hadley, President Emeritus of Yale University, entitled "Law-Making and Law Enforcement" and appearing in *Harper's Magazine* for November, 1925.

Who enforces the laws?

The first impulse of most people would be to answer, "The police and the sheriffs, with occasional assistance from the army in emergencies." But if we stop to think about the matter we shall see that this is a very superficial view of things and that only a small fraction of our law enforcement is secured or needs to be secured in this way. In ninety-nine cases out of a hundred obedience to the law is quite voluntary. The people at large do not have to be compelled by the police to obey the laws against murder or burglary or the various regulations for the convenience of the public. They do it of themselves, either as a matter of conscience or in deference to public opinion. And the fact that they do it of themselves is the thing which makes civilized society possible. It enables the police to concentrate their attention on the work of protecting the public against a relatively small number of habitual law-breakers who do not recognize their moral obligations to themselves or to society. Conscience and public opinion enforce the laws; the police suppress the exceptions.

What is this public opinion and how is it formed?

[3] Reprinted with the permission of the author and of the publishers, Harper and Brothers.

Man, as Aristotle well says, is a political animal. He has the impulse to make himself part of a social group; to accept the habits and the standards approved by the group, and to follow the traditional rules of conduct which it has adopted. In the early stages of society these standards and rules are imposed by the church and formulated by the priests. Public action is ordered by religious precepts; disobedience to those precepts is checked by the fear of the gods. As civilization advances, other institutions besides the church take their share in setting social standards. The school and the theater, the platform and the press, serve as agencies for shaping public sentiment and public ideals. The desire for the approval of our fellow men takes its place side by side with the fear of God as a motive for conforming to the demands of society. A man who habitually conforms to these demands without external compulsion is said to be law-abiding and public-spirited. When the great body of citizens is thus law-abiding and public-spirited the community is self-governing, in the true sense of the word. Its legislation and administration are founded on the principle set forth at the beginning of the Declaration of Independence, that the powers of a just government are derived from the consent of the governed.

To maintain this ideal political condition, two things are necessary. First, the great bulk of the members of society must be willing to go as far as public opinion demands without being compelled to do so by force; and second, the government authorities must be careful not to go beyond what public opinion demands in the laws which it makes or the acts which it requires. Every stable community has these two characteristics. The citizens are law-abiding; the officials are moderate in the exercise of their powers. Without the former we have anarchy; without the latter we have tyranny.

But some one will say, "This is obvious enough as far as a monarchy or aristocracy is concerned, where you have a ruler or ruling class on one side, trying to govern a people on the other. Such a community cannot be self-governing unless the king or nobles are strictly guided by public opinion. But how can democracy become a tyranny under any circumstances? Is not a democracy necessarily self-governing? Are not the acts of a democratic government, under certain prescribed rules which have been accepted as a constitution, necessarily expressions of what the majority of the people want?"

No. The citizens of a democracy are not necessarily self-governing. If we look at the history of different kinds of government, we shall find that officials elected by the people, whenever they have gained control of an army or police force large enough to carry out their mandates, have been just as frequently guilty of class discrimination, arbitrary arrest, or punishment without proper trial, as any monarch or any group of aristocrats. The very fact that a man has been elected to office by popular vote may lead him to cast self-restraint aside, and think that he is representing the people collectively when he tyrannizes over them individually. "Virtue," says Halévy, "is more dangerous than vice, because its excesses are not subject to the restraints of conscience."

Cromwell in England, Robespierre in France, Lenin in Russia, show how persistent is this danger in all races and conditions. Democracy has not meant self-government except when the rulers have shown self-restraint. . . .

One of the greatest dangers which now confront us is the increasing demand for ill-considered legislation, and the increasing readiness of would-be reformers to rely on authority rather than on public sentiment for securing their ends. When the republic was first founded, we had more to fear from the law-breakers than from the law-makers, from the absence of authority than from its over-exercise. People believed in individual liberty and even sometimes inclined to carry that idea to extremes. But this love of liberty has gradually given place to a zeal for standardization. The new democracy, in the words of Lord Farrer, is passionately benevolent and passionately fond of power. Today, it is from the law-maker rather than from the law-breaker that our American traditions of self-government have most to fear.

WHY SHOULD THE MAJORITY RULE? [4]

By Walter Lippmann

Walter Lippmann is an able writer on public questions. Formerly an editor of the *New Republic*, he is now in charge of the editorial page of the *New York World*. The excerpt below is from the chapter, "Bryan and the Dogma of Majority Rule" in his book, *Men of Destiny*.

[4] Reprinted by permission of and arrangement with the publishers, the Macmillan Company. Copyright, 1927.

Although the principle of majority rule derives a certain sanctity from the mystical sense of equality, it is really quite unrelated to it. There is nothing in the teachings of Jesus or St. Francis which justifies us in thinking that the opinions of 51 per cent. of a group are better than the opinions of 49 per cent. The mystical doctrine of equality ignores the standards of the world and recognizes each soul as unique; the principle of majority rule is a device for establishing standards of action in this world by the crude and obvious device of adding up voters. Yet owing to a confusion between the two, the mystical doctrine has been brutalized and made absurd, and the principle of majority rule has acquired an unction that protects it from criticism. A mere political expedient, worth using only when it is necessary or demonstrably useful to the conduct of affairs, has been hallowed by an altogether adventitious sanctity due to an association of ideas with a religious hope of salvation.

Once we succeed in disentangling this confusion of ideas, it becomes apparent that the principle of majority rule is wholly alien to what the humane mystic feels. The rule of the majority is the rule of force. For while nobody can seriously maintain that the greatest number must have the greatest wisdom or the greatest virtue, there is no denying that under modern social conditions they are likely to have the most power. I say likely to have, for we are reminded by the recent history of Russia and of Italy that organized and armed minorities can under certain circumstances disfranchise the majority. Nevertheless, it is a good working premise that in the long run the greater force resides in the greater number, and what we call a democratic society might be defined for certain purposes as one in which the majority is always prepared to put down a revolutionary minority.

The apologists of democracy have done their best to dissemble the true nature of majority rule. They have argued that by some mysterious process the opinion to which a majority subscribes is true and righteous. They have even attempted to endow the sovereign majority with the inspiration of an infallible church and of kings by the grace of God. It was a natural mistake. Although they saw clearly enough that the utterances of the church were the decisions of the ruling clergy, and that the divine guidance of the king was exercised by his courtiers, they were not prepared to admit that the new sovereign was a purely temporal ruler. They felt certain they must ascribe to the majority of the voters the same supernatural excellence which had always adhered to the traditional rulers. Throughout the nineteenth century, therefore, the people were flattered and mystified by hearing that deep within a fixed percentage of them there lay the same divine inspiration and the same gifts of revelation which men had attributed previously to the established authorities.

And then just as in the past men had invented a mythical ancestry for their king, tracing his line back to David or Aeneas or Zeus himself, so the minnesingers of democracy have invented their own account of the rise of popular government. The classic legend is to be found in the theory of the Social Contract, and few naïve democrats are without traces of belief in this legend. They imagine that somehow "the people" got together and established nations and governments and institutions. Yet the historic record plainly shows that the progress of democracy has consisted in an increasing participation of an increasing number of people in the management of institutions they neither created nor willed. And the record shows, too, that new numbers were allowed to participate when they were powerful enough to force their way in; they were enfranchised not because "society" sought the benefits of their wisdom, and not because "society" wished them to have power; they were enfranchised because they had power, and giving them the vote was the least disturbing way of letting them exercise their power. For the principle of majority rule is the mildest form in which the force of numbers can be exercised. It is a pacific substitute for civil war in which the opposing armies are counted and the victory is awarded to the larger before any blood is shed.

Except in the sacred tests of democracy and in the incantations of the orators, we hardly take the trouble to pretend that the rule of the majority is not at bottom a rule of force. What other virtue can there be in 51 per cent. except the brute fact that 51 is more than 49? The rule of 51 per cent. is a convenience; it is for certain matters a satisfactory political device, it is for others the lesser of two evils, and for still others it is accept-

able because we do not know any less troublesome
method of obtaining a political decision. But it may
easily become an absurd tyranny if we regard it wor-
shipfully, as though it were more than a political device.
We have lost all sense of its true meaning when we
imagine that the opinion of 51 per cent. is in some high
fashion the true opinion of the whole 100 per cent., or
indulge in the sophistry that the rule of a majority is
based upon the ultimate equality of man.

At Dayton Mr. Bryan contended that in schools sup-
ported by the state the majority of the voters had a
right to determine what should be taught. If my analysis
is correct, there is no fact from which that right can
be derived except the fact that the majority is stronger
than the minority. It cannot be argued that the majority
in Tennessee represented the whole people of Tennessee;
nor that fifty-one Tennesseeans are better than forty-
nine Tennesseeans; nor that they were better biologists,
or better Christians, or better parents, or better Americans. It cannot be said they are necessarily more in tune
with the ultimate judgments of God. All that can be said
for them is that there are more of them, and that in a
world ruled by force it may be necessary to defer to the
force they exercise.

When the majority exercises that force to destroy the
public schools, the minority may have to yield for a
time to this force, but there is no reason why they
should accept the result. For the votes of a majority
have no intrinsic bearing on the conduct of a school.
They are external facts to be taken into consideration

like the weather or the hazard of fire. Guidance for a school can come ultimately only from educators, and the question of what shall be taught as biology can be determined only by biologists. The votes of a majority do not settle anything here, and they are entitled to no respect whatever. They may be right, or they may be wrong; there is nothing in the majority principle which will make them either right or wrong. In the conduct of schools, and especially as to the details of the curriculum, the majority principle is an obvious irrelevance. It is not even a convenient device as it is in the determination, say, of who shall pay the taxes.

But what good is it to deny the competence of the majority when you have admitted that it has the power to enforce its decisions? I enter this denial myself because I prefer clarity to confusion, and the ascription of wisdom to 51 per cent. seems to me a pernicious confusion. But I do it also because I have some hope that the exorcising of the superstition which has become attached to majority rule will weaken its hold upon the popular imagination, and tend therefore to keep it within convenient limits. Mr. Bryan would not have won the logical victory he won at Dayton if educated people had not been caught in a tangle of ideas which made it seem as if the acknowledgment of the absolutism of the majority was necessary to faith in the final value of the human soul. It seems to me that a rigorous untangling of this confusion might help to arm the minority for a more effective resistance in the future.

AN INDICTMENT OF DEMOCRACY [5]
By *William Ralph Inge*

Dean William Ralph Inge, of St. Paul's Cathedral, London, brings to current problems one of the ablest and most stimulating minds in England today. His essays are marked by incisive and independent thinking. The matter quoted is from the discussion, "Our Present Discontents," in his *Outspoken Essays*, First Series.

Democracy is a form of government which may be rationally defended, not as being good, but as being less bad than any other. Its strongest merits seem to be: first, that the citizens of a democracy have a sense of proprietorship and responsibility in public affairs, which in times of crisis may add to their tenacity and endurance. The determination of the Federals in the American Civil War, and of the French and British in the four years' struggle against Germany, may be legitimately adduced as arguments for democracy. When Tocqueville says that "it is hard for a democracy to begin or to end a war," the second is truer than the first. And, secondly, the educational value of democracy is so great that it may be held to counterbalance many defects. Mill decides in favor of democracy mainly on the ground that "it promotes a better and higher form of national character than any other polity," since government by authority stunts the intellect, narrows the sympathies, and destroys the power of initiative. "The perfect commonwealth," says Mr.

[5] Reprinted by permission of and arrangement with the publishers, Longmans, Green, and Company.

Zimmern, "is a society of free men and women, each at once ruling and being ruled." It is also fair to argue that monarchies do not escape the worst evils of democracies. An autocracy is often obliged to oppress the educated classes and to propitiate the mob. Domitian massacred senators with impunity, and only fell *post-quam cerdonibus esse timendus coeperat*. If an autocracy does not rest on the army, which leads to the chaos of praetorianism, it must rely on *panem et circenses*. Hence it has some of the worst faults of democracy, without its advantages. As Mr. Graham Wallas says: "When a tsar or a bureaucracy finds itself forced to govern in opposition to a vague national feeling which may at any moment create an overwhelming national purpose, the autocrat becomes the most unscrupulous of demagogues, and stirs up racial or religious or social hatred, or the lust for foreign war, with less scruple than a newspaper proprietor under a democracy." The autocrat, in fact, is often a slave, as the demagogue is often a tyrant. Lastly, the democrat may urge that one of the commonest accusations against democracy—that the populace chooses its rulers badly—is not true in times of great national danger. On the contrary, it often shows a sound instinct in finding the strongest man to carry it through a crisis. At such times the parrots and monkeys are discarded, and a Napoleon or a Kitchener is given a free hand, though he may have despised all the demagogic arts. In other words, a democracy sometimes knows when to abdicate. The excesses of revolutionists are not an argument against democracy, since revolutions are anything rather than democratic.

Nevertheless, the indictment against democracy is a very heavy one, and it is worth while to state the main items in the charge.

1. Whatever may be truly said about the good sense of a democracy during a great crisis, at ordinary times it does not bring the best men to the top. Professor Hearnshaw, in his admirable *Democracy at the Crossroads*, collects a number of weighty opinions confirming this judgment. Carlyle, who proclaimed the merits of silence in some thirty volumes, blamed democracy for ignoring the "noble, silent men" who could serve it best, and placing power in the hands of windbags. Ruskin, Matthew Arnold, Sir James Stephen, Sir Henry Maine, and Lecky, all agree that "the people have for the most part neither the will nor the power to find out the best men to lead them." In France the denunciations of democratic politicians are so general that it would be tedious to enumerate the writers who have uttered them. One example will suffice; the words are the words of Anatole Leroy-Beaulieu in 1885:

"The wider the circle from which politicians and state-functionaries are recruited, the lower seems their intellectual level to have sunk. This deterioration in the personnel of government has been yet more striking from the moral point of view. Politics have tended to become more corrupt, more debased, and to soil the hands of those who take part in them and the men who get their living by them. Political battles have become too bitter and too vulgar not to have inspired aversion in the noblest and most upright natures by their vio-

lence and their intrigues. The élite of the nation in more
than one country are showing a tendency to have nothing to do with them. Politics is an industry in which a
man, to prosper, requires less intelligence and knowledge
than boldness and capacity for intrigue. It has already
become in some states the most ignominious of careers.
Parties are syndicates for exploitation, and its forms
become ever more shameless."

2. The democracy is a ready victim to shibboleths
and catch-words, as all demagogues know too well. "The
abstract idea," as Schérer says, "is the national aliment
of popular rhetoric, the fatal form of thought which, for
want of solid knowledge, operates in a vacuum." The
politician has only to find a fascinating formula; facts
and arguments are powerless against it. The art of the
demagogue is the art of the parrot; he must utter some
senseless catch-word again and again, working on the
suggestibility of the crowd. Archbishop Trench, *On the
Study of Words*, notices this fact of psychology and the
use which is commonly made of it:

"If I wanted any further evidence of the moral atmosphere which words diffuse, I would ask you to observe how the first thing men do, when engaged in controversy with others, is ever to assume some honorable
name to themselves, such as, if possible, shall beg the
whole subject in dispute, and at the same time to affix
on their adversaries a name which shall place them in a
ridiculous or contemptible or odious light. A deep instinct, deeper perhaps than men give any account of to
themselves, tells them how far this will go; that multi-

tudes, utterly unable to weigh the arguments on one side
or the other, will yet be receptive of the influences
which these words are evermore, however imperceptibly,
diffusing. By argument they might hope to gain over the
reason of a few, but by help of these nicknames the
prejudices and passions of the many."

The chief instrument of this base art is no longer the
public speech but the newspaper.

The psychology of the crowd has been much studied
lately, by Le Bon and other writers in France, by Mr.
Graham Wallas in England. I think that Le Bon is in
danger of making the Crowd a mystical, superhuman
entity. Of course, a crowd is made up of individuals,
who remain individuals still. We must not accept the
stuffed idol of Rousseau and the socialists, "the General Will," and turn it into an evil spirit. There is no
General Will. All we have a right to say is that individuals are occasionally guided by reason, crowds never.

3. Several critics of democracy have accused it not
only of rash iconoclasm, but of obstinate conservatism
and obstructiveness. It seems unreasonable to charge the
same persons with two opposite faults; but it is true
that where the popular emotions are not touched, the
masses will cling to old abuses from mere force of habit.
As Maine says, universal suffrage would have prohibited
the spinning-jenny and the power-loom, the threshing-
machine and the Gregorian calendar; and it would have
restored the Stuarts. The theory of democracy—*vox
populi vox dei*—is a pure superstition, a belief in a divine
or natural sanction which does not exist. And supersti-

tion is usually obstructive. "We erect the temporary watchwords of evanescent politics into eternal truths; and having accepted as platitudes the paradoxes of our fathers, we perpetuate them as obstacles to the progress of our children." [6]

4. A more serious danger is that of vexatious and inquisitive tyranny. This is exercised partly through public opinion, a vulgar, impertinent, anonymous tyrant who deliberately makes life unpleasant for any one who is not content to be the average man. But partly it is seen in constant interference with the legislature and the executive. No one can govern who cannot afford to be unpopular, and no democratic official can afford to be unpopular. Sometimes he has to wink at flagrant injustice and oppression; at other times a fanatical agitation compels him to pass laws which forbid the citizen to indulge perfectly harmless tastes, or tax him to contribute to the pleasures of the majority. In many ways a Russian under the tsars was far less interfered with than an Englishman or American or Australian.

5. But the two diseases which are likely to be fatal to democracy are anarchy and corruption. A democratic government is almost necessarily weak and timid. A democracy cannot tolerate a strong executive for fear of seeing the control pass out of the hands of the mob. The executive must be unarmed and defenseless. The result is that it is at the mercy of any violent and anti-social faction. . . .

6. The corruption of democracies proceeds directly

[6] *Times Literary Supplement*, London, July 18, 1918.

from the fact that one class imposes the taxes and another class pays them. The constitutional principle, "No taxation without representation," is utterly set at nought under a system which leaves certain classes without any effective representation at all. At the present time it is said that one-tenth of the population pays five-sixths of the taxes. The class which imposes the taxes has refused to touch the burden of the war with one of its fingers; and every month new doles at the public expense are distributed under the camouflage of "social reform." At every election the worldly goods of the minority are put up to auction. This is far more immoral than the old-fashioned election bribery, which was a comparatively honest deal between two persons; and in its effects it is far more ruinous. Democracy is likely to perish, like the monarchy of Louis XVI, through national bankruptcy.

Besides these defects, the democracy has ethical standards of its own, which differ widely from those of the educated classes. Among the poor, "generosity ranks far before justice, sympathy before truth, love before chastity, a pliant and obliging disposition before a rigidly honest one. In brief, the less admixture of intellect required for the practice of any virtue, the higher it stands in popular estimation."[7] In this country, at any rate, democracy means a victory of sentiment over reason. Some may prefer the softer type of character, and may hope that it will make civilization more humane and compassionate than it has been in the past.

[7] Miss M. Loane. Mr. Stephen Reynolds has said the same.

Unfortunately, experience shows that none is so cruel as the disillusioned sentimentalist. He thinks that he can break or ignore nature's laws with impunity; and then, when he finds that nature has no sentiment, he rages like a mad dog, and combines with his theoretical objection to capital punishment a lust to murder all who disagree with him. This is the genesis of Jacobinism and Bolshevism.

But whether we think that the bad in democracy predominates over the good, or the good over the bad, a question which I shall not attempt to decide, the popular balderdash about it corresponds to no real conviction. The upper class has never believed in it; the middle class has the strongest reasons to hate and fear it. But how about the lower class, in whose interests the whole machine is supposed to have been set going? The workingman has no respect for either democracy or liberty. His whole interest is in transferring the wealth of the minority to his own pocket. There was a time when he thought that universal suffrage would get for him what he desires; but he has lost all faith in constitutional methods. To levy blackmail on the community, under threats of civil war, seems to him a more expeditious way of gaining his object. Monopolies are to be established by pitiless coercion of those who wish to keep their freedom. The trade unions are large capitalists; they are well able to start factories for themselves and work them for their own exclusive profit. But they find it more profitable to hold the nation to ransom by blockading the supply of the necessaries of life. The new laborer despises productivity for the same reason that the old robber barons did: it is less trouble to take money than to make it. The most outspoken popular leaders no longer conceal their contempt for and rejection of democracy. The socialists perceive the irreconcilable contradiction between the two ideas, and they are right. Democracy postulates community of interest or loyal patriotism. When these are absent it cannot long exist. Syndicalism, which seems to be growing, is the antipodes of socialism, but, like socialism, it can make no terms with democracy. "If syndicalism triumphs," says its chief prophet Sorel, "the parliamentary régime, so dear to the intellectuals, will be at an end." "The syndicalist has a contempt for the vulgar idea of democracy; the vast unconscious mass is not to be taken into account when the minority wishes to act so as to benefit it." [8] "The effect of political majorities," says Mr. Levine, "is to hinder advance." Accordingly, political methods are rejected with contempt. The anarchists go one step further. Bakunin proclaims that "we reject all legislation, all authority, and all influence, even when it has proceeded from universal suffrage." These powerful movements, opposed as they are to each other, agree in spurning the very idea of democracy, which Lord Morley defines as government by public opinion, and which may be defined with more precision as direct government by the votes of the majority among the adult members of a nation. Even a political philosopher

[8] A. D. Lewis, *Syndicalism and the General Strike.*

like Mr. Lowes Dickinson says, "For my part, I am no democrat."

Who then are the friends of this *curieux fétiche*, as Quinet called democracy? It appears to have none, though it has been the subject of factuous laudation ever since the time of Rousseau. The Americans burn incense before it, but they are themselves ruled by the Boss and the Trust.

THE ABLEMAN

By *Thomas Carlyle*

Thomas Carlyle had little confidence in democracy, believing that it signified mediocrity. Find the *able* man, put him in power—that will be the salvation of mankind. This theme is woven in and out of his *Heroes and Hero Worship*. The brief quotation below is from *The Hero as King*.

We come now to the last form of Heroism; that which we call Kingship. The Commander over Men; he to whose will our wills are to be subordinated, and loyally surrender themselves, and find their welfare in doing so, may be reckoned the most important of Great Men. He is practically the summary for us of *all* the various figures of Heroism; Priest, Teacher, whatsoever of earthly or of spiritual dignity we can fancy to reside in a man, embodies itself here, to *command* over us, to furnish us with constant practical teaching, to tell us for the day and hour what we are to *do*. He is called *Rex*, Regulator, *Roi*: our own name is still better; King, *Könning*, which means *Can*-ning, Able-man.

Numerous considerations, pointing toward deep,

questionable, and indeed unfathomable regions, present themselves here: on the most of which we must resolutely for the present forbear to speak at all. As Burke said that perhaps fair *Trial by Jury* was the soul of Government, and that all legislation, administration, parliamentary debating, and the rest of it, went on, in "order to bring twelve impartial men into a jury-box"—so, by much stronger reason, may I say here, that the finding of your *Ableman* and getting him invested with the *symbols of ability*, with dignity, worship (*worth*ship), royalty, kinghood, or whatever we call it, so that *he* may actually have room to guide according to his faculty of doing it—is the business, well or ill accomplished, of all social procedure whatsoever in this world! Hustings-speeches, Parliamentary motions, Reform Bills, French Revolutions, all mean at heart this; or else nothing. Find in any country the Ablest Man that exists there; raise *him* to the supreme place, and loyally reverence him: you have a perfect government for that country; no ballot-box, parliamentary eloquence, voting, constitution-building, or other machinery whatsoever can improve it a whit. It is in the perfect state; an ideal country. The Ablest Man; he means also the truest-hearted, justest, the Noblest Man: what he *tells us to do* must be precisely the wisest, fittest, that we could anywhere or anyhow learn—the thing which it will in all ways behove us, with right loyal thankfulness, and nothing doubting, to do! Our *doing* and life were then, so far as government could regulate it, well regulated; that were the ideal of constitutions.

THE GLORY OF THE MEDIAEVAL [9]

By Ralph Adams Cram

Ralph Adams Cram is an architect, living in Boston, and
the author of a number of books on subjects related to his
field. He is preëminently a mediaevalist, believing that there
was a beauty and simplicity in the life of mediaeval Europe
that forms a striking contrast to what he considers the artificial, crowded, and cheap life of our own day. Like Carlyle,
he finds democracy inseparable from mediocrity, and believes
it incapable of lifting itself out of its vulgarity. The quotation is from the Prologue of his little book, *Walled Towns*.

The stone-flagged path on the top of the high walls
winds along within the battlemented parapet, broken
here and there by round turrets, steeple-crowned barriers of big timbers, and, at wider intervals, great
towers, round or square or many-sided, where bright
banners blow in the unsullied air. From one side you
may look down on and into the dim city, jostling the
ramparts with crowding walls and dizzy roofs, from the
other the granite scarp drops sheer to the green fields
and vari-colored gardens and shadowy orchards full
forty feet below.

Within, the city opens up in kaleidoscopic vistas as
you walk slowly around the walls; here are the steep
roofs of tall houses with delicate dormers, fantastic
chimney stacks, turret cupolas with swinging weather
vanes; here the closed gardens of rich burgesses, full of
arbors, flowers, pleached alleys of roses, *espaliers* of pear
and nectarine; here a convent or guild chapel, newly

[9] Reprinted with the permission of the publishers, the Marshall Jones
Company.

worked of yellow stone and all embroidered with the garniture of niches, balustrades, and pinnacles. Here, under one of the city gates, opens a main street, narrow and winding but walled with high-gabled houses, each story jutting beyond the lower, carved from pavement to ridge like an Indian jewel casket, and all bedecked with flaming color and burnished gold-leaf. Below is the stream and eddy of human life; craftsmen in the red and blue and yellow of their guild liveries, slow-pacing merchants and burghers in furred gowns of cramoisy and Flemish wool and gold-woven Eastern silks; scholars in tippet and gown, youths in slashed doublets and gay hose, gray friars and black and brown, with a tonsured monk or two, and perhaps a purple prelate, attended, and made way for with deep reverence. Threading the narrow road rides a great lady on a gayly caparisoned palfrey, with an officious squire in attendance, or perhaps a knight in silver armor, crested wonderfully, his emblazoned shield hanging at his saddle-bow—living color mixing and changing between leaning walls of still color and red gold.

Here a stream or canal cuts the houses in halves, a quay with gay booths and markets of vari-colored vegetables along one side, walls of pink brick or silvery stone on the other, jutting oriels hanging over the stream, and high, curved bridges, each with its painted shrine, crossing here and there, with gaudy boats shoving along underneath. Here a square opens out, ringed with carved houses—a huge guild hall on one side, with its dizzy watch-tower where hang the great alarum bells; long rows of Gothic arches, tall mullioned windows, and tiers and ranges of niched statues all gold and gules and azure, painted perhaps by Messer Jan Van Eyck or Messer Hans Memling. In the center is a spurting fountain with its gilt figures and chiseled parapet, and all around are market booths with bright awnings where you may buy strange things from far lands, chaffering with dark men from Syria and Saracen Spain and Poland and Venice and Muscovy.

And everywhere, tall in the midst of tall towers and spires, vast silvery, light as air, yet solemn and dominating, the great shape of the Cathedral, buttressed, pinnacled, beautiful with rose windows and innumerable figures of saints and angels and prophets.

There is no smoke and no noxious gas; the wind that sweeps over the roofs and around the delicate spires is as clean and clear as it is in the mountains; the painted banners flap and strain, and the trees in the gardens rustle beneath. There is no sound except human sound; the stir and murmur of passing feet, the pleasant clamor of voices, the muffled chanting of cloistered nuns in some veiled chapel, the shrill cry of street venders and children, and the multitudinous bells sounding for worship in monastery or church and, at dawn and noon and evening, the answering clangor of each to all for the Angelus.

And from the farther side of the walls a wide country of green and gold and the far, thin blue of level horizon or distant mountains. There are no slums and no suburbs and no mills and no railway yards; the green fields and the yellow grain, the orchards and gardens and thickets of trees sweep up to the very walls, slashed by winding white roads. Alongside the river, limpid and unstained, are mills with slow wheels dripping quietly, there where the great bridge with its seven Gothic arches and its guarding towers curves in a long arc from shore to shore. Far away is perhaps a gray monastery with its tall towers, and on the hill a grayer castle looming out of the woods. Along the road blue-clad peasants come and go with swaying flocks of sheep and fowl and cattle. Here are dusty pilgrims with staff and wallet and broad hats, pursy merchants on heavy horses with harness of red velvet and gold embroidery; a squadron of mounted soldiers with lances and banners, and perhaps my Lord Bishop on his white mule, surrounded by his retainers, and on progress to his see city from some episcopal visitation; perhaps even a plumed and visored knight riding on quest or to join a new Crusade to the Holy Land.

Color everywhere, in the fresh country, in the carven houses, in gilded shrines and flapping banners, in the clothes of the people like a covey of vari-colored tropical birds. No din of noise, no pall of smoke, but fresh air blowing within the city and without, even through the narrow streets, none too clean at best, but cleaner far than they were to be thereafter and for many long centuries to come.

Such was any walled town in the fifteenth century, let us say in France or England or Italy, in Flanders or Spain or the Rhineland. Carcassonne, Rothenburg, San Gimignano, Oxford, ghosts of the past, arouse haunt-ings of memory today, but they tell us little, for the color is gone, and the stillness and the clean air. Ghosts they are and not living things; and life, color, clarity, these were the outward marks of the Walled Towns of the Middle Ages.

"It was not a pretty station where McCann found himself, and he glared ill-naturedly around with restless, aggressive eyes. The brick walls, the cheaply grained doors bearing their tarnished legends, 'Gents,' 'Ladies,' 'Refreshment Saloon,' the rough-raftered roof over the tracks—everything was black and grimy with years of smoke, belching even now from the big locomotive, and gathering like an ill-conditioned thunder-cloud over the mob of scurrying, pushing men and women, a mob that swelled and scattered constantly in fretful confusion. A hustling business-man with a fat, pink face and long sandy whiskers, his silk hat cocked on one side in grotesque assumption of jauntiness, tripped over the clay-covered pick of a surly laborer, red of face and sweaty, blue of overalls and mud-colored of shirt, and as he stumbled over the annoying implement, scowled coarsely, and swore, with his cigar between his teeth.

"Ragged and grimy children, hardly old enough to walk, sprawled and scrambled on the dirty platform, and as McCann hurried by, a five-year-old cursed shrilly a still more youthful little tough, who answered in kind. Vulgar theater-bills in rank reds and yellows flaunted on the cindery walls; discarded newspapers, banana skins, cigar butts, and saliva were ground together vilely under foot by the scuffling mob. Dirt, meanness, ugliness everywhere—in the unhappy people no less than in their surroundings. . . .

"The prospect was not much better outside than in. The air was thick with fine white dust, and dazzling with fierce sunlight. On one side was a wall of brick tenements, with liquor saloons, cheap groceries, and a fish-market below, all adding their mite to the virulence of the dead, stifling air. Above, men in dirty shirt-sleeves lolled out of the grimy windows, where long festoons of half-washed clothes drooped sordidly. On the other side, gangs of workmen were hurriedly repairing the ravages of a fire that evidently had swept clear a large space in its well-meant but ineffectual attempts at purgation. Gaunt black chimneys wound with writhing gas-pipes, tottering fragments of wall blistered white on one side, piles of crumbling bricks where men worked sullenly loading blue carts, mingled with new work, where the walls, girdled with yellow scaffolding, were rising higher, uglier than before; the plain factory walls with their rows of square windows less hideous by far than those buildings where some ignorant contractor was trying by the aid of galvanized iron to produce an effect of tawdry, lying magnificence. Dump-carts, market-wagons, shabby hacks, crawled or scurried along in the hot dust. A huge dray loaded with iron bars jolted over the granite pavement with a clanging, clattering din that was maddening. In fact, none of the adjuncts of a thriving progressive town were absent, so far as one could see. . . .

"The carriage threaded its way through the roaring crowd of vehicles, passing the business part of the city, and entering a tract given over to the factories, hideous blocks of barren brick and shabby clapboards, through the open windows of which came the brain-killing whir of heavy machinery, and hot puffs of oily air. Here and there would be small areas between the buildings where foul streams of waste from some factory of cheap calico would mingle dirtily with pools of green, stagnant water, the edges barred with stripes of horrible pinks and purples where the water had dried under the fierce sun. All around lay piles of refuse—iron hoops, broken bottles, barrels, cans, old leather, stewing and fuming in the dead heat, and everywhere escape-pipes vomited steam in spurts. Over it all was the roar of industrial civilization. McCann cast a pitying look at the pale, dispirited figures passing languidly to and fro in the midst of the din and the foul air, and set his teeth closely.

"Presently they entered that part of the city where live the poor, they who work in the mills, when they are not on a strike, or the mills are not shut down—as barren of trees or grass as the center of the city, and the baked gray earth trodden hard between the crowded tenements painted lifeless grays, as dead in color as the clay about them. Children and goats crawled starvedly around or huddled in the hot shadow of the sides of the houses. This passed, and then came the circle of 'suburban residences,' as crowded almost as the tottering tenements, but with green grass around them.

Frightful spectacles these,—'Queen Anne' and 'Colonial' vagaries painted lurid colors, and frantic in their cheap elaboration. Between two affected little cottages painted orange and green and with round towers on their corners, stood a new six-story apartment-house with vulgar front of brown stone, 'Romanesque' in style, but with long flat sides of cheap brick. McCann caught the name on the big white board that announced 'Suites to Let,' 'Hotel Plantagenet,' and grinned savagely.

"Then, at last, even this region of speculative horrors came to an end, giving place to a wide country road that grew more and more beautiful as they left the town far behind. McCann's eyebrows were knotted in a scowl. The ghastly nonsense, like a horrible practical joke, that the city had been to him, excited, as it always did, all the antagonism within his rebellious nature. Slowly and grimly he said to himself, yet half aloud, in a tone of deliberation, as though he were cursing solemnly the town he had left: 'I hope from my soul that I may live to see the day when that damned city will be a desolate wilderness; when those chimneys shall rise smokeless; when those streets shall be stony valleys between grisly ridges of fallen brick; when Nature itself shall shrink from repairing the evil that man has wrought; when the wild birds shall sweep widely around that desolation that they may not pass above; when only rats and small snakes shall crawl through the ruin of that "thriving commercial and manufacturing metropolis"; when the very name it bore in the days of its dirty glory shall have become a synonym for horror and despair!' Having thus relieved himself he laughed softly, and felt better." [10]

THE NEMESIS OF MEDIOCRITY [11]

By Ralph Adams Cram

Democratic government for the last twenty-five years has neither desired nor created leaders of an intellectual or moral capacity above that of the general mass of voters, and when by chance these appear they are abandoned for a type that is not of the numerical average but below it, and the standard has been lowering itself steadily for a generation. The strong man, strong of mind, of will, of moral sense, the man born to create and to lead, now seeks other fields for his activity, or rather one field alone, and that the field of "big business" and finance. Here at least he finds scope for his force and will and leadership, even if the opportunities to use his moral sense to advantage leave something to be desired. The world no longer wants or knows how to use statesmen, philosophers, artists, religious prophets, and shepherds, but rather "captains of industry," directors of "high finance," "efficiency experts," shrewd manipulators of popular opinion through journalism, or of popular vote through primaries, political conventions, and the legislative chambers of representative government. Here also the demand creates the supply.

[10] *The Decadent,* 1893.
[11] Reprinted from the book of the same title, with the permission of the publishers, the Marshall Jones Company.

Tributary to this demand is the current system of popular education, probably the worst ever devised so far as character-making is concerned. Secularized, eclectic, vocational, and intensive educational systems do not educate in any true sense of the word, while they do not develop character, but even work in the opposite direction. The concrete results of popular education, as this has been conducted during the last generation, have been less and less satisfactory both from the point of view of culture and that of character, and the product of schools and colleges tends steadily toward a lower and lower level of attainment. Why anything else should be expected is hard to see. The new education, with religion and morals ignored except under the aspect of archeology; with Latin and Greek superseded, and all other cultural studies as well; with logic, philosophy, and dialectic abandoned for psychology, biology, and "business administration"; the new education with its free electives and vocational training, and its apotheosis of theoretical and applied science (a glory and a dominion mitigated only by the insidious penetration of semi-professional athletics)—this new education was conceived and put in practice for the chief purpose of fitting men for the sort of life that was universal during the lapsed years of the present century, and this life had no place for preëminence, no use for leadership, except in the categories of business, applied science, and finance. It did its work to admiration, and the result is before us in the shape of a society that has been wholly democratized, not by filling in the valleys and lifting the

selected

malarial swamps of the submerged masses, but by a leveling of all down to their own plane. . . .

Democracy, without the supreme leadership of men who by nature or divine direction can speak and act with and by authority, is a greater menace than autocracy. Men and nations have been what they have been, either for good or evil, not by the will of the numerical majority but by the supreme leadership of the few—seers, prophets, captains of men; and so it will always be. When, as now, the greatest crisis of fifteen centuries overpasses the world, and society sinks under the Nemesis of universal mediocrity, then we realize that the system has doomed itself, since, impotent to produce leaders, it has signed its own death-warrant.

INTELLECTUAL LIFE IN A DEMOCRACY [12]

By Harold E. Stearns

Such an atmosphere [one of fraternal democracy] will become as infested with cranks, fanatics, mushroom religious enthusiasts, moral prigs with new schemes of perfectibility, inventors of perpetual motion, illiterate novelists, and oratorical cretins, as a swamp with mosquitoes. They seem to breed almost overnight; we have no standard to which the wise and the foolish may equally repair, no criterion by which spontaneously to appraise them and thus, by robbing them of the breath of their life, recognition, reduce their numbers. On the

[12] From "The Intellectual Life," in *Civilization in the United States*, by Thirty Americans. Reprinted here with the permission of the publishers, Harcourt, Brace and Company.

contrary, we welcome them all with a kind of Jamesian gusto, as if every fool, like every citizen, must have his right to vote. It is a kind of intellectual enfranchisement that produces the same sort of leadership which, in the political field of complete suffrage, we suffer under from Washington and our various state capitols. Our intellectual life, when we judge it objectively on the side of vigor and diversity, too often seems like a democracy of mountebanks.

THE LAZY LEVEL OF THE AVERAGE [13]

By Rabindranath Tagore

In an article entitled "East to West," appearing in the *Atlantic Monthly* for June, 1927, Rabindranath Tagore, poet and prophet of India, comments upon our Western democracy.

While aristocracy strenuously cultivates self-respect, often at the cost of material profit, and guards a high standard of culture against deterioration, undiluted democracy has a tendency to glide down to the lazy level of the average, for all its striving is to add to its rights, not to build up a high tower of excellence. It makes a deliberate study of the laws of the dark patches in the human intellect, wherewith to help itself to create an atmosphere of delusion through hints, gestures, yells, and startling grimaces, for the purpose of stupefying the popular mind. Once when I was in Chicago I saw everywhere on the town walls one single name blazoned in big letters in an endless round of repetition, like the

[13] Reprinted with the permission of the *Atlantic Monthly*.

whirling monotony of a dervish dance that dazes one's mind into vacuity. Evidently the name belonged to some candidate for political election. But what an insult to the people, who are supposed to represent the supreme power in their government, openly to apply to them the spell of hypnotism in place of reason, as the medicine-man does in the heart of Africa!

A DEFENSE OF DEMOCRACY [14]

By Edwin Grant Conklin

In the face of the strong indictment of democracy, Edwin Grant Conklin, professor of zoölogy at Princeton University, still finds any government except that of the people intoler-able, and he believes that, whatever their deficiencies, the people have resources within themselves to work out their salvation. The material presented here is drawn from his book, *The Direction of Human Evolution*.

Can democracy save itself from the serious faults and dangers which threaten it? Can the people, as a whole, be trusted to choose wisely their leaders and policies? Can the democratic ideals of liberty, equality, and fra-ternity bring about that rational coöperation upon which the further progress of society must depend? No man can answer these questions now with certainty, but at least it can be said that no other system of social organization which has yet been tried holds so much promise of success.

The rational powers of the masses of mankind are

[14] Reprinted with the permission of the publishers, Charles Scribner's Sons.

not very great, and if the success of democracy depended upon human reason alone, the prospect would not be very encouraging. Although Lincoln's saying is true that "you can fool all of the people some of the time, and some of the people all of the time, but you cannot fool all of the people all of the time," nevertheless if a majority of the people can be fooled most of the time the outlook for future democracy would not be very bright, if progress depended solely upon the rational powers of mankind.

But the firm foundations upon which democracy rests go deeper than the intellect and reason of man; they go down to the instincts and emotions and moral judgments which underlie all social evolution. Upon these foundations the rational organization of society stands as a splendid but still insecure superstructure.

The moral judgments of men may be no better than their practical judgments, but judgment which is founded upon much experience, even if it be based on so low a level as "trial and error," is generally sound. Out of the conflict of opinion and ideals of multitudes of persons in all walks and circumstances of life there comes at last a compromise or adjustment which we call "common sense" and which has the pragmatic quality of viability.

Although we cannot always trust the rational processes of the people as a whole, it is the creed of democracy that we can trust their social instincts and moral judgments. Their instincts of service and sympathy, and their judgments as to right and wrong, as to justice and injustice, are the bases upon which the ideals of liberty, equality, and fraternity rest. These instincts and judgments are so deep-seated and so widespread, that they form a firm foundation for democracy.

All students of mankind have based their hopes of democracy upon these instincts and judgments, and no one has expressed this thought more forcefully than President Wilson. In his address at Independence Hall on July 4, 1914, he said: "The way to success in this great country, with its fair judgments, is to show that you are not afraid of anybody except God and his final verdict. If I did not believe that, I would not believe in democracy. If I did not believe that, I would not believe that people can govern themselves. If I did not believe that the moral judgment would be the last judgment, the final judgment in the minds of men as well as the tribunal of God, I could not believe in popular government. But I do believe these things, and, therefore, I earnestly believe in the democracy, not only of America, but of every awakened people that wishes and intends to govern and control its own affairs." And in his address to the American Bar Association on October 20, 1914, he said: "You cannot go any faster than you can advance the average moral judgments of the mass; but you can go at least as fast as that, and you can see to it that you do not lag behind the average moral judgments of the mass. I have in my life dealt with all sorts and conditions of men, and I have found that the flame of moral judgment burned just as bright in the man of humble life and limited experience as in the scholar and the man of affairs." Upon these instincts and judgments which are deeply planted in the nature and heart of humankind rest the present successes and the future hopes of democracy.

DISCUSSION AND THEME TOPICS

1. In the course of your life from day to day as a member of society are you conscious of being seriously interfered with by any existing law, by any loyalty to the interests of a group, by the dictates of custom or the force of popular opinion? Is your life set about by obstructions which prevent its natural expression? Would your personal desire, for instance, lead you to commit one of the following acts?

   a. To strike your neighbor, whom you detest, when you happen to meet him on the street.

   b. To write and publish an account, which you believe to be a truthful record, of his vicious and deceitful life, so that the world may know him as he is.

   c. To enter a bank and take securities (presuming you have the opportunity) to the amount of what you have been previously defrauded by the sharp practice of some of the bank officials.

   d. To ignore the quarantine restrictions of a Board of Health which you regard as stupidly officious.

   If you have desires in these directions, you cannot express them without conflict with the law of the land. Obviously your personal liberty is destroyed by forces outside of yourself. You cannot perform what may seem to you a supremely righteous act, which the gods themselves might applaud.

   Write an account of your personal experience in a world of regulation and law, showing what your attitude is toward it all. Are you inwardly rebellious, or for the most part indifferent, or does your logical thinking bring you to conformity? What would happen if you actually lived the life you set your heart upon?

2. Imagine that you are the editor of a small city paper. Write an editorial in which you discuss for your readers the question of law and their relation to it. It would perhaps be well to take as your starting-point some incident which has occurred in the community, similar to those suggested above, and proceed from that to a discussion of general principles involved, seeking to establish a working basis of community conduct.

3. Imagine that you are in a state or community in which legislation has recently come into force which you regard as the product of ignorant and bigoted thinking on the part of the law-makers and the people who put them in power. The law which has been enacted affects your personal conduct, and you resent its authority.

   a. Write an open letter to the editor of your paper, clearly and vigorously, but in a dignified fashion, setting forth your protest against laws which you deem highly unwise, and arguing your right to disregard the rule of the unenlightened majority.

   b. Write the editor's reply to this open letter, in which he defends the reign of law and the sacredness of a statute once on the books, such a respect for law being, in his opinion, the only basis upon which government can continue to exist.

4. Imagine for the moment that you are the president of some college or university and that the question has arisen of the advisability of granting freedom of the platform to a certain speaker whose views are extreme and very much at odds with the more or less established thought of the college. Protests against his coming have been received from various prominent people of the state and from organizations of influence. The decision rests finally in your hands. Think the matter out and prepare a statement for the press in which you announce your decision, and set forth clearly the course of reasoning which has led to your conclusion. Present the whole problem with intelligence and sincerity and if possible in

such a way as to indicate a future policy for the college while it is under your direction.

5. Watch the crowds on the street of a Saturday night or in the rush hours of the subway or at the movies or at a labor meeting or a "big revival," and say to yourself: "These are the people who elect our legislators and officers of government; these are the voters who will mark out a nation's destiny. For America is a democracy, and the 'people' rule." Then write an editorial in which you discuss democracies and what they do. Present the picture with hope or with misgiving. Write vividly and with conviction, if you can, and lift your style out of the ordinary, not, of course, by added ornament, but by the simplicity and vigor of your thought.

SUGGESTIONS FOR MORE EXTENDED STUDY

1. Read Walter Lippmann's book, *Men of Destiny*, from which one of the selections in this chapter was taken. Mr. Lippmann discusses with vivid interest men and problems of our day. From this reading make an analysis of the author's general viewpoint and of his application of it to our "American scene."

2. Make a somewhat extended study of the rule of the majority, and embody your observations and conclusions in a paper of some length. Is the rule of the majority "at bottom a rule of force"? Is there no other virtue in 51 per cent. than the "brute fact that 51 is more than 49? Most people accept without demur majority rule as the guiding factor of the common life, for the direction of education, legislation, and the various society controls. As you consider the question, jot down points that seem significant, and note specific illustrations of their application. Your material will grow as you think the problem through. Organize the ideas which you have before you, elaborate some points, discard others, search for apt illustrations and effective phrasings. Write it all out in a paper of some length.

3. Read and make a critical review of any one of the various books suggested for parallel reading with this chapter—books from the pens of thinkers who win the attention of the thoughtful public everywhere. Discover what the essential thing is that each one is saying; set that forth; and then discuss, as you can, its measure of truth. Some reading will be more difficult than other reading, but if you make the mental effort you will be surprised and happy to see your mind growing constantly in power.

4. Write a criticism of Mr. Cram's method of drawing the contrasted pictures of medieval and modern civilizations. Is it done with fairness? Or do you feel that he had a thesis to establish and selected his details to that end? If you believe that he distorted the picture and manipulated his materials, see if you cannot, in turn, by a different selection of details, produce a contrast which will be favorable to our present-day life.

5. John Stuart Mill feared that democracy might tend to become a system which would compel individuals to think and act in the same way, thus forming a distinct barrier to human progress. Sir J. F. Stephen in his *Liberty, Fraternity, and Equality* (1874) replied to Mill's essay on liberty and maintained that a democracy could be trusted to take care of its own liberties. Write a critical analysis of Stephen's argument.

VOCABULARY LIST

servile	valid	postulate
propriety	provocation	syndicalism
apprehend	propagation	sophisticate
coercion	refuted	heterodox
illegitimate	rational	waive
noxious	erroneous	tenable
hypothesis	corrigible	forensic
devolve	collating	plausible
dissentient	cognizant	mandate
pernicious	gainsayer	expedient
incumbent	monopoly	adventitious

mystic
disfranchise
premise
dissemble
apologist
minnesinger
naïve
pacific
incantation
sophistry
ultimate
antipodes
fatuous
laudation
intrinsic
irrelevance
exorcising
bureaucracy
unscrupulous

syndicate
exploitation
ignominious
odious
iconoclasm
entity
evanescent
platitude
paradox
flagrant
camouflage
pliant
impunity
balderdash
blackmail
expeditious
battlemented
scarp
kaleidoscopic

vista
tonsured
caparisoned
oriel
chaffer
mullioned
covey
limpid
secularize
eclectic
mitigate
apotheosis
insidious
category
viability
dithyrambic
disaffection
autocracy

READING LIST

The list comprises the sources from which the selections in the text are taken, and other works bearing upon the discussion of the chapter.

John Stuart Mill. *On Liberty.*

James C. Carter. *Law: Its Origin, Growth, and Function.* New York, 1907.

James Bryce. *Modern Democracies.* New York, 1921.

Arthur Twining Hadley. "Law-Making and Law-Enforcement." *Harper's Magazine,* November, 1925.

Walter Lippmann. *Men of Destiny.* New York, 1927.

William Ralph Inge. *Outspoken Essays.* London. First Series, 1920; Second Series, 1922.

Thomas Carlyle. *Heroes and Hero-Worship.*

Ralph Adams Cram. *The Nemesis of Mediocrity.* Boston, 1917.
——*Walled Towns.* Boston, 1919.
——*Sins of the Fathers.* Boston, 1919.

Harold E. Stearns. "The Intellectual Life." In *Civilization in the United States*, by Thirty Americans. New York, 1922.

Rabindranath Tagore. "East to West." *Atlantic Monthly*, June, 1927.

Edwin G. Conklin. *The Direction of Human Evolution*. New York, 1921.

Henry Adams. *The Degradation of the Democratic Dogma*. New York, 1919.

John Dewey. *Democracy and Education*. New York, 1916.

Irving Babbitt. *Democracy and Leadership*. Boston, 1924.

Everett Dean Martin. *The Behavior of Crowds*. New York, 1920.

J. B. Bury. *A History of Freedom of Thought*. New York, 1913.

Gerald Stanley Lee. *Crowds*. New York, 1914.

H. M. Kallen. *Culture and Democracy in the United States*. New York, 1924.

Chapter V

THE IDEA OF PROGRESS; THE OLD AND THE NEW; THE SEARCH FOR THE ENDURING GOOD

In the foregoing chapters we have made inquiry concerning the nature of man's thought-processes, his prejudices and convictions, his search for enduring standards of excellence, the crystallizing of the opinion of the compact majority and the revolt of the individual against its domination, and the growing distrust of democracy. All this leads inevitably to the paramount question: In the midst of complexity and seeming confusion, is any course or direction discernible, is there progress toward some ultimate goal? Whither is civilization tending? Is advancement or degradation the law of the universe? Or is all change nought but ebb and flow, endlessly repeated? As we watch century dissolve into century, civilizations come to birth, flourish, and die, as we see our age yielding inevitably to a new era whose nature we can but dimly guess, we ponder the fate that is in store for the race.

For man is the universe come to consciousness. After untold eons, Nature has at last evolved a product with capacity to observe her never-resting labors. With man's appearance on the earth, the curtain lifted, as it were, on the drama of the ages, and the play is now going on before human eyes. It is a play concerned with the processes of immeasurable time, and it dwarfs into nothingness the episodes of daily existence. If we can succeed in gaining an intelligent perspective and view the drama as a whole, we shall see how irresistible is the driving power of progress, how eager the pursuit of the unrealized goal, and yet how varied are the paths by which different people, different civilizations, have sought to gain the enduring good. In our own age, it is science, perhaps, more than anything else, that is holding out to man the glowing hope of attainment. Many thinkers, however, appraising at a low value the contributions of a physical world, look within themselves for sources of enduring satisfaction, building a temple of the mind in which to worship. Some urge a return to the simpler life and emotions of the Middle Ages. Others, relinquishing hope for any happy destiny of mankind, seek escape for themselves in a world of beauty, in the pleasure of sensation, in religious experience, or in philosophical resignation, a denial of the will to live. It may well be that the important occupation of man is a search for a philosophy of life which will enable him to meet the circumstances of his existence with understanding and fortitude.

Toward an intelligent orientation, let us examine divergent viewpoints of various thinkers of our day.

THE IDEA OF PROGRESS [1]

By *William Ralph Inge*

The following discussion is taken from the *Outspoken Essays*, Second Series, of Dean Inge.

The belief in Progress, not as an ideal but as an indisputable fact, not as a task for humanity but as a law of Nature, has been the working faith of the West for about a hundred and fifty years. Some would have us believe that it is a long-neglected part of the Christian revelation, others that it is a modern discovery. The ancient pagans, we are told, put their Golden Age in the past; we put ours in the future. The Greeks prided themselves on being the degenerate descendants of gods, we on being the very creditable descendants of monkeys. The Romans endeavored to preserve the wisdom and virtue of the past, we to anticipate the wisdom and virtue of the future. This, however, is an exaggeration. The theory of progress and the theory of decadence are equally natural, and have in fact been held concurrently wherever men have speculated about their origin, their present condition, and their future prospects. Among the Jews the theory of decadence derived an inspired authority from Genesis, but the story of the Fall had very little influence upon the thought of that tenaciously optimistic race. Among the Greeks, who had the melancholy as well as the buoyancy of youth, it was authorized by Hesiod, whose scheme of retrogression

[1] Reprinted by permission of and arrangement with the publishers, Longmans, Green, and Company.

from the age of gold to the age of iron was never forgotten in antiquity. Sophocles, in a well-known chorus imitated by Bacon, holds that the best fate for men is "not to be born, or being born to die. . . ." But the deepest thought of antiquity was neither optimistic nor pessimistic. It was that progress and retrogression are only the incoming and outgoing tide in an unchanging sea. The pulse of the universe beats in an alternate expansion and contraction. The result is a series of cycles, in which history repeats itself. Plato contemplates a world-cycle of 36,000 solar years, during which the Creator guides the course of events; after which he relaxes his hold of the machine, and a period of the same length follows during which the world gradually degenerates. When this process is complete the Creator restores again the original conditions, and a new cycle begins. Aristotle thinks that all the arts and sciences have been discovered and lost "an infinite number of times." Virgil in the Fourth *Eclog* tries to please Augustus by predicting the near approach of a new Golden Age, which, he says, is now due. This doctrine of recurrence is not popular today; but whether we like it or not, no other view of the macrocosm is even tenable. Even if those physicists are right who hold that the universe is running down like a clock, that belief postulates a moment in past time when the clock was wound up; and whatever power wound it up once may presumably wind it up again. The doctrine of cycles was held by Goethe, who, in reply to Eckermann's remark that "the progress of humanity seems to be a matter of thousands of years," answered:

"Perhaps of millions. Men will become more clever and discerning, but not better or happier, except for limited periods. I see the time coming when God will take no more pleasure in our race, and must again proceed to a rejuvenated creation. I am sure that the time and hour in the distant future are already fixed for the beginning of this epoch. But we can still for thousands of years enjoy ourselves on this dear old playground of ours. . . ."

The Dark Ages knew that they were dark, and we hear little talk about progress during those seven centuries which, as far as we can see, might have been cut out of history without any great loss to posterity. The Middle Ages (which we ought never to confuse with the Dark Ages), though they developed an interesting type of civilization, set their hopes mainly on another world. The Church has never encouraged the belief that this world is steadily improving; the Middle Ages, like the early Christians, would have been quite content to see the earthly career of the race closed in their own time. Even Roger Bacon, who is claimed as the precursor of modern science, says that all wise men believe that we are not far from the time of Antichrist, which was to be the herald of the end. The Renaissance was a conscious recovery from the longest and dreariest setback that humanity has ever experienced within the historical period—a veritable glacial age of the spirit. At this time men were too full of admiration and reverence for the

newly recovered treasures of antiquity to look forward
to the future. In the seventeenth century a doctrine of
progress was already in the air, and a long literary battle
was waged between the Ancients and the Moderns. But
it was only in the eighteenth century that Western
Europe began to dream of an approaching millennium
without miracle, to be gradually ushered in under the
auspices of a faculty which was called Reason. Unlike
some of their successors, these optimists believed that
perfection was to be attained by the self-determination
of the human will; they were not fatalists. In France,
the chief home of this heady doctrine, the psychical
temperature soon began to rise under its influence, till
it culminated in the delirium of the Terror. The God-
dess of Reason hardly survived Robespierre and his
guillotine; but the belief in progress, which might
otherwise have subsided when the French resumed their
traditional pursuits—*rem militarem et argute loqui*—
was reënforced by the industrial revolution, which was
to run a very different course from that indicated by
the theatrical disturbances at Paris between 1789 and
1794, the importance of which has perhaps been exag-
gerated. In England above all, the home of the new
industry, progress was regarded (in the words which
Mr. Mallock puts into the mouth of a nineteenth-century scientist) as that kind of improvement which can
be measured by statistics. This was quite seriously the
view of the last century generally, and there has never
been, nor will there ever be again, such an opportunity
for gloating over this kind of improvement. The me-

chanical inventions of Watt, Arkwright, Crompton,
Stephenson, and others led to an unparalleled increase
of population. Exports and imports also progressed, in
a favorite phrase of the time, by leaps and bounds.
Those who, like Malthus, sounded a note of warning,
showing that population increases, unlike the supply of
food, by geometrical progression, were answered that
compound interest follows the same admirable law. It
was obvious to many of our grandparents that a nation
which travels sixty miles an hour must be five times as
civilized as one which travels only twelve, and that, as
Glanvill had already declared in the reign of Charles II,
we owe more gratitude to the inventor of the mariner's
compass "than to a thousand Alexanders and Cæsars,
or to ten times the number of Aristotles." The historians
of the time could not contain their glee in recording
these triumphs. Only the language of religion seemed
appropriate in contemplating so magnificent a spectacle.
If they had read Herder, they would have quoted with
approval his prediction that "the flower of humanity,
captive still in its germ, will blossom out one day into
the true form of man like unto God, in a state of which
no man on earth can imagine the greatness and the
majesty." Determinism was much in vogue by this time;
but why should determinism be a depressing creed?
The law which we cannot escape is the blessed law of
progress—"that kind of improvement that can be
measured by statistics." We had only to thank our stars
for placing us in such an environment, and to carry out
energetically the course of development which Nature

has prescribed for us, and to resist which would be at once impious and futile.

Thus the superstition of progress was firmly established. To become a popular religion, it is only necessary for a superstition to enslave a philosophy. The superstition of progress had the singular good fortune to enslave at least three philosophies—those of Hegel, of Comte, and of Darwin. The strange thing is that none of these philosophies is really favorable to the belief which it was supposed to support. Leaving for the present the German and the French thinkers, we observe with astonishment that many leading men in Queen Victoria's reign found it possible to use the great biological discovery of Darwin to tyrannize over the minds of their contemporaries, to give their blessing to the economic and social movements of their time, and to unite determinism with teleology in the highly edifying manner to which I have already referred. Scientific optimism was no doubt rampant before Darwin. For example, Herschel says: "Man's progress toward a higher state need never fear a check, but must continue till the very last existence of history." But Herbert Spencer asserts the perfectibility of man with an assurance which makes us gasp. "Progress is not an accident but a necessity. What we call evil and immorality must disappear. It is certain that man must become perfect." "The ultimate development of the ideal man is certain —as certain as any conclusion in which we place the most implicit faith; for instance, that all men will die." "Always toward perfection is the mighty movement—

toward a complete development and a more unmixed good. . . ."

The racial life of the species to which we happen to belong is a brief episode even in the brief life of the planet. And what we call civilization or culture, though much older than we used to suppose, is a brief episode in the life of our race. For tens of thousands of years the changes in our habits must have been very slight, and chiefly those which were forced upon our rude ancestors by changes of climate. Then in certain districts man began, as Samuel Butler says, to wish to live beyond his income. This was the beginning of the vast series of inventions which have made our life so complex. And, we used to be told, the "law of all progress is the same, the evolution of the simple into the complex by successive differentiations." This is the gospel according to Herbert Spencer. As a universal law of nature, it is ludicrously untrue. Some species have survived by becoming more complex, others, like the whole tribe of parasites, by becoming more simple. On the whole, perhaps the parasites have had the best of it. The progressive species have in many cases flourished for a while and then paid the supreme penalty. The living dreadnoughts of the Saurian age have left us their bones, but no progeny. But the microbes, one of which had the honor of killing Alexander the Great at the age of thirty-two, and so changing the course of history, survive and flourish. The microbe illustrates the wisdom of the maxim, λάθε βιώσας. It took thousands of years to find him out. Our own species, being rather poorly provided by nature for offense and defense, had to live by its wits, and so came to the top. It developed many new needs, and set itself many insoluble problems. Physiologists like Metchnikoff have shown how very ill-adapted our bodies are to the tasks which we impose upon them; and in spite of the Spencerian identification of complexity with progress, our surgeons try to simplify our structure by forcibly removing various organs which they assure us that we do not need. If we turn to history for a confirmation of the Spencerian doctrine, we find, on the contrary, that civilization is a disease which is almost invariably fatal, unless its course is checked in time. The Hindus and Chinese, after advancing to a certain point, were content to mark time; and they survive. But the Greeks and Romans are gone; and aristocracies everywhere die out. Do we not see today the complex organization of the ecclesiastic and college don succumbing before the simple squeezing and sucking apparatus of the profiteer and trade-unionist? If so-called civilized nations show any protracted vitality, it is because they are only civilized at the top. Ancient civilizations were destroyed by imported barbarians; we breed our own. . . .

It was impossible that such shallow optimism as that of Herbert Spencer should not arouse protests from other scientific thinkers. Hartmann had already shown how a system of pessimism, resembling that of Schopenhauer, may be built upon the foundation of evolutionary science. And in this place we are not likely to forget the second Romanes Lecture, when Professor Huxley

astonished his friends and opponents alike by throwing
down the gauntlet in the face of Nature, and bidding
mankind to find salvation by accepting for itself the
position which the early Christian writer Hippolytus
gives as a definition of the Devil—"he who resists
the cosmic process" ('σάντιτάττων τοις κοσμικοις).
The revolt was not in reality so sudden as some of Huxley's hearers supposed. He had already realized that "so
far from gradual progress forming any necessary part
of the Darwinian creed, it appears to us that it is perfectly consistent with indefinite persistence in one state,
or with a gradual retrogression. Suppose, e.g., a return
of the glacial period or a spread of polar climatical conditions over the whole globe." The alliance between determinism and optimism was thus dissolved; and as
time went on, Huxley began to see in the cosmic process
something like a power of evil. The natural process, he
told us in this place, has no tendency to bring about the
good of mankind. Cosmic nature is no school of virtue,
but the headquarters of the enemy of ethical nature.
Nature is the realm of tiger-rights; it has no morals and
no ought-to-be; its only rights are brutal powers. Morality exists only in the "artificial" moral world: man is
a glorious rebel, a Prometheus defying Zeus. This strange
rebound into Manicheism sounded like a blasphemy
against all the gods whom the lecturer was believed to
worship, and half-scandalized even the clerics in his
audience. It was bound to raise the question whether this
titanic revolt against the cosmic process has any chance
of success. One recent thinker, who accepts Huxley's

view that the nature of things is cruel and immoral, is willing to face the probability that we cannot resist it with any prospect of victory. Mr. Bertrand Russell, in his arresting essay, "A Free Man's Worship," shows us Prometheus again, but Prometheus chained to the rock and still hurling defiance against God. He proclaims the moral bankruptcy of naturalism, which he yet holds to be forced upon us:

"That man is the product of causes which had no prevision of the end they were achieving; that his origin, his growth, his hopes and fears, his loves and his beliefs, are but the outcome of accidental collocations of atoms; that no fire, no heroism, no intensity of thought and feeling, can preserve an individual beyond the grave; that all the labors of the ages, all the devotion, all the inspiration, all the noonday brightness of human genius, are destined to extinction in the vast death of the solar system, and that the whole temple of man's achievement must inevitably be buried beneath the débris of a universe in ruins—all these things, if not quite beyond dispute, are yet so nearly certain, that no philosophy which rejects them can hope to stand. Only within the scaffolding of these truths, only on the firm foundation of unyielding despair, can the soul's habitation henceforth be safely built."

Man belongs to "an alien and inhuman world," alone amid "hostile forces." What is man to do? The God who exists is evil; the God whom we can worship is the creation of our own conscience, and has no existence outside it. The "free man" will worship the latter; and, like John Stuart Mill, "to hell he will go."

If I wished to criticize this defiant pronouncement, which is not without a touch of bravado, I should say that so complete a separation of the real from the ideal is impossible, and that the choice which the writer offers us, of worshiping a Devil who exists or a God who does not, is no real choice, since we cannot worship either. But my object in quoting from this essay is to show how completely naturalism has severed its alliance with optimism and belief in progress. Professor Huxley and Mr. Russell have sung their palinode and smashed the old gods of their creed. No more proof is needed, I think, that the alleged law of progress has no scientific basis whatever.

But the superstition has also invaded and vitiated our history, our political science, our philosophy, and our religion.

The historian is a natural snob; he sides with the gods against Cato, and approves the winning side. He lectures the vanquished for their willfulness and want of foresight, sometimes rather prematurely, as when Seeley, looking about for an example of perverse refusal to recognize facts, exclaims, "*Sedet, aeternumque sedebit* unhappy Poland!" The nineteenth-century historian was so loath to admit retrogression that he liked to fancy the river of progress flowing underground all through the Dark Ages, and endowed the German barbarians who overthrew Mediterranean civilization with all the manly virtues. If a nation, or a religion, or a school of art dies, the historian explains why it was not worthy to live.

In political science the corruption of the scientific spirit by the superstition of progress has been flagrant. It enables the disputant to overbear questions of right and wrong by confident prediction, a method which has the double advantage of being peculiarly irritating and incapable of refutation. On the theory of progress, what is "coming" must be right. Forms of government and modes of thought which for the time being are not in favor are assumed to have been permanently left behind. A student of history who believed in cyclical changes and long swings of the pendulum would take a very different and probably much sounder view of contemporary affairs. The votaries of progress mistake the flowing tide for the river of eternity, and when the tide turns they are likely to be left stranded like the corks and scraps of seaweed which mark the high-water line. This has already happened, though few realize it. The praises of Liberty are mainly left to Conservatives, who couple it with Property as something to be defended, and to conscientious objectors, who dissociate it from their country, which is not to be defended. Democracy —the magic ballot-box—has few worshipers any longer except in America, where men will still shout for about two hours—and indeed much longer—that she is "great." . . .

It is easy to criticize the forms which Hope has assumed. But the Hope which has generated them is a solid fact, and we have to recognize its indomitable tenacity and power of taking new shapes. The belief in a law of progress, which I have criticized so unmercifully, is one of these forms; and if I am not mistaken, it is nearly worn out. Disraeli in his detached way said, "The European talks of progress because by the aid of a few scientific discoveries he has established a society which has mistaken comfort for civilization." It would not be easy to sum up better the achievements of the nineteenth century, which will be always remembered as the century of accumulation and expansion. It was one of the great ages of the world; and its greatness was bound up with that very idea of progress which, in the crude forms which it usually assumed, we have seen to be an illusion. It was a strenuous, not a self-indulgent age. The profits of industry were not squandered, but turned into new capital, providing new markets and employment for more labor. The nation, as an aggregate, increased in wealth, numbers, and power every day; and public opinion approved this increase, and the sacrifices which it involved. It was a great century; there were giants in the earth in those days; I have no patience with the pygmies who gird at them. But, as its greatest and most representative poet said:

"God fulfills himself in many ways,
Lest one good custom should corrupt the world."

The mold in which the Victorian age cast its hopes is broken. There is no law of progress; and the gains of that age now seem to some of us to have been purchased too high, or even to be themselves of doubtful value. In

Clough's fine poem, beginning "Hope evermore and believe, O man," a poem in which the ethics of Puritanism find their perfect expression, the poet exhorts us:

"Go! say not in thine heart, And what then, were it accomplished,
Were the wild impulse allayed, what were the use and the good?"

But this question, which the blind Puritan asceticism resolutely thrust on one side, has begun to press for an answer. It had begun to press for an answer before the great cataclysm, which shattered the material symbols of the cult which for a century and a half had absorbed the chief energies of mankind. Whether our widespread discontent is mainly caused, as I sometimes think, by the unnatural conditions of life in large towns, or by the decay of the ideal itself, is not easy to say. In any case, the gods of Queen Victoria's reign are no longer worshiped. And I believe that the dissatisfaction with things as they are is caused not only by the failure of nineteenth-century civilization, but partly also by its success. We no longer wish to progress on those lines if we could. Our apocalyptic dream is vanishing into thin air. It may be that the industrial revolution which began in the reign of George III has produced most of its fruits, and has had its day. We may have to look forward to such a change as is imagined by Anatole France at the end of his *Island of Penguins*, when, after an orgy of revolution and destruction, we shall slide back into the quiet rural life of the early modern period. If so, the authors of the revolution will have cut their own throats, for there can be no great manufacturing towns in such a society. The race will have tried a great experiment, and will have rejected it as unsatisfying. . . .

The laws of Nature neither promise progress nor forbid it. We could do much to determine our own future; but there has been no consistency about our aspirations, and we have frequently followed false lights, and been disillusioned as much by success as by failure. The well-known law that all institutions carry with them the seeds of their own dissolution is not so much an illustration of the law of cyclical revolution, as a proof that we have been carried to and fro by every wind of doctrine. What we need is a fixed and absolute standard of values, that we may know what we want to get and whither we want to go. It is no answer to say that all values are relative and ought to change. Some values are not relative but absolute. Spiritual progress must be within the sphere of a reality which is not itself progressing, or for which, in Milton's grand words, "progresses the dateless and irrevoluble circle of its own perfection, joining inseparable hands with joy and bliss in over-measure for ever." Assuredly there must be advance in our apprehension of the ideal, which can never be fully realized because it belongs to the eternal world. We count not ourselves to have apprehended in aspiration any more than in practice. As Nicolas of Cusa says: "To be able to know ever more and more without end, this is our likeness to the eternal Wisdom. Man always desires to know better what he knows, and to love more what he loves; and the whole world is not sufficient for him, because it does not satisfy his craving for knowledge." But since our object is to enter within the realm of unchanging perfection, finite and relative progress cannot be our ultimate aim, and such progress, like everything else most worth having, must not be aimed at too directly. Our ultimate aim is to live in the knowledge and enjoyment of the absolute values, Truth, Goodness, and Beauty. If the Platonists are right, we shall shape our surroundings more effectively by this kind of idealism than by adopting the creed and the methods of secularism. I have suggested that our disappointments have been very largely due to the unworthiness of our ideals, and to the confused manner in which we have set them before our minds. The best men and women do not seem to be subject to this confusion. So far as they can make their environment, it is a society immensely in advance of anything which has been realized among mankind generally.

If any social amelioration is to be hoped for, its main characteristic will probably be simplification rather than further complexity. This, however, is not a question which can be handled at the end of a lecture.

Plato says of his ideal state that it does not much matter whether it is ever realized on earth or not. The type is laid up in heaven, and approximations to it will be made from time to time, since all living creatures are drawn upward toward the source of their being. It does not matter very much, if he was right in believing

—as we too believe—in human immortality. And yet it does matter; for unless our communing with the eternal Ideas endows us with some creative virtue, some power which makes itself felt upon our immediate environment, it cannot be that we have made those Ideas in any sense our own. There is no alchemy by which we may get golden conduct out of leaden instincts—so Herbert Spencer told us very truly; but if our ideals are of gold, there is an alchemy which will transmute our external activities, so that our contributions to the spiritual temple may be no longer "wood, hay, and stubble," to be destroyed in the next conflagration, but precious and durable material.

For individuals, then, the path of progress is always open; but, as Hesiod told us long before the Sermon on the Mount, it is a narrow path, steep and difficult, especially at first. There will never be a crowd gathered round this gate; "few there be that find it." For this reason, we must cut down our hopes for our nation, for Europe, and for humanity at large, to a very modest and humble aspiration. We have no millennium to look forward to; but neither need we fear any protracted or widespread retrogression. There will be new types of achievement which will enrich the experience of the race; and from time to time, in the long vista which science seems to promise us, there will be new flowering-times of genius and virtue, not less glorious than the age of Sophocles or the age of Shakespeare. They will not merely repeat the triumphs of the past, but will add new varieties to the achievements of the human mind.

Whether the human type itself is capable of further physical, intellectual, or moral improvement, we do not know. It is safe to predict that we shall go on hoping, though our recent hopes have ended in disappointment. Our lower ambitions partly succeed and partly fail, and never wholly satisfy us; of our more worthy visions for our race we may perhaps cherish the faith that no pure hope can ever wither, except that a purer may grow out of its roots.

THE CYCLIC LAW OF PROGRESS [2]

By Ralph Adams Cram

This material is taken from Mr. Cram's little book, *The Decadent* (1893), from which we have already quoted.

"Oh, that law of evolution—I knew that you would quote it to me sooner or later. You hug the pleasant and cheerful theory to your hearts, and twist history to fit its fancied laws. You cannot see that the law of evolution works by a system of waves advancing and retreating; yet as you say, the tide goes forward always. Civilizations have risen and fallen in the past as ours has risen and is falling now. Does history repeat itself? Can you not see that it is one of the periods of decadence that alternate inevitably with the periods of advance? The tide—

[2] Reprinted with the permission of the publishers, the Marshall Jones Company.

" 'Was once, too, at the full, and round earth's shore
   Lay like the folds of a bright girdle furl'd.
   But now I only hear
   Its melancholy, long, withdrawing roar,
   Retreating to the breath
   Of the night-wind, down the vast edges drear
   And naked shingles of the world.'

"Yes, it is the decadence, the Roman decadence over
again. Were Lucian to come among us now he would be
quite at ease—no, not that, for in one thing we are utterly changed; so sordid is our decadence, so gross, so
contemptibly material, that we are denied the consola-
tions of art vouchsafed to his own land. Even in the
days of her death Rome could boast the splendor of a
luxuriant literature, the glory of beauty of environment, the supremacy of an art-appreciation that blinded
men's eyes to the shadow of the end. But for us, in the
measure of our fall, we have no rags of art wherewith
to cover our nakedness. Wagner is dead, and Turner and
Rossetti; Burne-Jones and Watts will go soon, and Pater
will follow Newman and Arnold. The night is at hand."

He lifted a small hammer and struck a velvet-voiced
bell that stood on an Arabian table of cedar inlaid with
nacre and ivory. Murad came out of the darkness, and
at a gesture from Aurelian filled the great hookah of
jade and amber with the tobacco mingled with honey
and opium and cinnamon, placed a bright coal in the
cup and gave the curling stem wound with gold thread
to his master.

PROGRESS THROUGH SCIENCE [3]

By *Albert Edward Wiggam*

Mr. Wiggam, in his interesting and suggestive book, *The New Decalogue of Science,* calls attention to the important, if not controlling, part that the laws of science, and particularly the laws of biological science, play in determining the destiny of man. The knowledge which modern study and investigation have brought, constitutes an instrument which man can use to achieve mastery over the forces of nature. The old Greek slave cried out to his fellows, "Why call ye upon the gods? Ye have hands? Wipe your own nose." Mr. Wiggam suggests that the science laboratory may have a large contribution to make to the wisdom of statesmanship. The following quotation constitutes the introductory chapter in Mr. Wiggam's book. It bears the title, "The New Biology and the Old Statesmanship."

To His Excellency, The Statesman, Executive Mansion

Sir: Biology, as your Excellency I fear is only vaguely aware, is the science of life. It is what we know of living things.

Statesmanship, as you are fully aware, is the art—and we hope may some day be the science—of the control of life.

Now, you control life upon a vaster scale than any other human being. In every field of administration of those affairs which lie beyond individual control, whether in business, industry, education, religion, or politics proper, you are the chiefest arbiter of the destiny

[3] From the *New Decalogue of Science.* Copyright, 1923. Used by special permission of and arrangement with the publishers, the Bobbs-Merrill Company.

of the race. More than any other member of the community you determine who shall secure food, and who shall starve; who shall secure clothing and shelter, and who shall freeze; who shall obtain life's opportunities —its education, its social and economic rewards, and who, in these respects, shall fail; in short, who shall survive and who shall perish in the struggle for existence. In a real sense you determine the very trend of human evolution. What you think, therefore, and say and do about life, is the most important thing in the whole world.

Yet, your Excellency, I venture to address you personally in these pages, because there are now on the shelves of our libraries at least five or six thousand volumes and special investigations dealing with this subject of life of which, I regret to say, it seems you have never even heard. They represent the experiments upon life, and the best thinking of many of the world's greatest minds and noblest spirits for the past one hundred years. Since your own task is so extremely difficult and since you are dealing with precisely the same problem as are these men, it would seem that you could be of mutual service. You could immensely aid the biologist, and he believes that, after a hundred years of toil, he is now able to aid you. Every act of yours is freighted with such incalculable human destiny that it would seem, in ordinary humanness, of which your heart is so full, that you, your colleagues, your cabinets, chancelleries, legislators, would all be waiting with bated breath for every one of these great new insights into nature and human nature, these new solutions of your own most pressing problems, to pour from the laboratory.

Above all, when you witness daily the marvelous benefits in comfort, food, clothing, shelter, transportation, wealth, health, and longevity, which science in all its forms has brought to you and to your constituents, it would seem that you would seek earnestly to adopt for your own work at least the spirit and method, the life and viewpoint by which all these blessings have been achieved. Their danger lies in that they may increase the speed of life but not its tide and volume, its movement but not its cubic content, its swiftness but not its momentum. If you do not gather this new spirit and method, if you do not then apply it with decision and intelligence not only to wealth but to life, science, instead of bringing Utopia, will surely bring chaos. All this sense of progress will be merely a biological joyride with hell at the next turn. If I am mistaken in saying that you have never even heard of these numerous volumes about life, I am not mistaken, I think, in saying that they have had singularly slight influence upon your policy and action.

Your public utterances, but not your political, economic, or social structure and procedure, reveal, however, that you are familiar with some Ten Commandments which God wrote on tables of stone and gave to one of your predecessors as the true chart of statesmanship. He later added two supplements known as the Golden Rule and the Sermon on the Mount. Though you know them well, you have failed conspicuously to put these nourishing principles into practice; but what I think will surprise your Excellency is, to learn that God is still doing the same thing. However, in our day, instead of using tables of stone, burning bushes, prophecies, and dreams to reveal his will, he has given men the microscope, the spectroscope, the telescope, the chemist's test-tube, and the statistician's curve in order to enable men to make their own revelations. These instruments of divine revelation have not only added an enormous range of new commandments—an entirely new Decalogue—to man's moral codes, but they have supplied him with the technique for putting the old ones into effect.

Men have never been really righteous, because they did not know how. They could not obey God's will because they had no way of finding out what it was. The spirit of the old commandment to love thy neighbor as thyself was right, but how could a man love his neighbor intelligently when he did not know what was good for him? The good Samaritan bound up his fellow traveler's wounds, but doubtless left them full of microbes and thus probably killed him. The good Samaritan on the road to Jericho and the good Samaritan on Broadway live in two different moral worlds. "Give a cup of cold water to your neighbor" was a precious admonition, but modern science sternly asks, "Are there any colon bacilli in it?" "Multiply and replenish the earth" was a counsel of perfection when there were only eight people on the globe, but when there are two thousand millions it gives even the rhapsodist pause.

Especially, the biologist would like to know what sort of stock the earth is to be replenished with. He has found that many who multiply the most have not sufficient intelligence to add. And so one could run through all the great new categories of modern conduct. Your own imagination will suggest that the range of ancient moralities for a tribe can not suffice for the ethics of a planet. Not only that, the biologist has discovered that often apparently the noblest ethics for the born, work disaster to the unborn. It is not a personal nor tribal nor immediate morality, but a planetary, cosmic, generational, protoplasmic ethics that alone will make men really righteous.

It is, therefore, no extravagant assumption but the surest deduction from science itself that science only can supply mankind with the true technology of the will of God. If his will is ever to be done on earth as it is in Heaven, it will have to be done through the instrumentalities of science; that is, through the use of intelligence. Conscience will have to look through the microscope if it ever sees its duty aright. The most earnest sense of duty will not supply men with the true objectives of that duty. The "spirit of Christ," which we are glibly told will suffice for salvation, is majestic in its impulse and in its objective, but sadly lacking in any technique for connecting the two. It points truly the "steep and thorny path to Heaven," but it supplies no engineering details for making the ascent.

In fact man is either on his way to new scenes and changes, new varieties of untried being, or else he is in

fearful danger of falling into naught. For as old Cato
cried from his prison walls, "If there be a power above
us, and that there is, all nature cries aloud through all
her works, he must delight in virtue. And what he delights in must be happy." But again he cries, "When or
where?" Science answers, "Here and now, or nowhere
and never." This world was not, as Cato said, "made
for Cæsar." It was made for the common man. Indeed, so far as science knows, this world was not made
for anything. It simply is. It is simply here for this organic creature man, himself, who is the outcome of its
multitudinous but friendly forces, to make it a congenial decent home to live in, love in, marry in, rear his
children in, and die in. So far, except in limited areas
and for brief moments for a few people, it has never
been fit for any of these things. For most people it has
been merely a place to fight and freeze and starve in,
with a snatch now and then of wine and poetry and
song. It may always be so. It may be that man's only
hope is to "grunt and sweat under a weary life" on the
bare hazard that another world will right the ills of this.
But science is lighting the world with a different faith,
a belief founded on knowledge, that this world, too, can
be made clean and sane and happy. If man can not clean
up this world with the stupendous cosmic engine of
science now in his hands, he does not deserve another.
He will have to receive it as a pittance because some-
body else "atoned" for his foolishness.

But the scientist can not be daunted with the failure
of one generation or even one age. He looks to the long

results of time. His old geology has taught him patience. But he believes that man will cease looking solely to the hills which the Psalmist intimated were his only source of help, and look closer about him and within him into his own psychology and biology in order to aid whatever help may come from on high. This does not mean necessarily that what lies upon and beyond those hills has ceased to stretch a friendly hand to the heart that trusts them. The scientist knows that beyond them are many things not within his ken. He knows, as the mystic can not know, that beyond them lie nobler mysteries and finer adventures of the spirit than the mystic has ever dreamed. But the things that lie beyond he believes are as friendly as those he has found on this side. Consequently, without troubling, he trusts them. He believes they are on the side of intelligence. Instead of believing that religion is merely "morality touched with emotion," and that such a religion will furnish a ready-made science of society, he believes that intelligence touched with emotion is the only guide to morality. That kind of morality touched with emotion is religion. And that kind of religion and only that kind will induce men to clean up this world, instead of letting its filth accumulate in the belief that man's stay here below is too short for it to be worth while to make the place decent. Men have been dominated by this belief for ages, with the obvious result that religion and morality have scarcely progressed beyond the Stone Age. We are still in the Stone Age of ethics. As John Dewey in substance asks, where is our science of society—our moral adjustments of men to one another—comparable to our progress in chemistry or physics? There simply is no such progress, there is no science of society, because men have not known how to behave toward one another—have not known until this age of science how to be righteous.

But at last, your Excellency, men do know how to be good. Science has supplied them with a true technique of righteousness. The time has arrived for a new Decalogue, a new Sermon on the Mount, a new Golden Rule. These new codes of conduct have none of the absolutism of the old. They are fluid as evolution, flexible as human nature. Yet the new dispensation is just as divine, as sacred, as inspired as the old. It is filled with warnings of wrath, both present and to come, for the biological ungodly, as well as with alluring promises for them who do his scientific will. These warnings should first make you tremble; they should, secondly, make you pray; they should, thirdly, fill you with the militant faith of a new evangel.

PROGRESS THROUGH REVOLT AND CHANGE

It is the belief of many that the secret of progress lies in the field of ideas. Without a repudiation of the mass of ignorance and error that have belonged to the past, there can be no growth. Such people place their confidence in a germinal energy which they find in the new age. Others regard with suspicion the constant

clamor for change; to them it is the mark of the effer-
vescing and unstable mind.

DISILLUSION AND PROGRESS [4]

By H. L. Mencken and R. R. LaMonte

I conceive progress as a sort of process of disillusion.
Man gets ahead, in other words, by discarding the theory
of today for the fact of tomorrow. . . . The mob is
inert and moves ahead only when it is dragged or driven.
It clings to its delusions with a pertinacity that is ap-
palling. A geological epoch is required to rid it of a
single error, and it is so helpless and cowardly that every
fresh boon it receives . . . must come to it as a free
gift from its betters, as a gift not only free but
forced. . . .

What virtues do I demand in the man who claims
enrollment in the highest caste? Briefly, I demand that
he possess, to an unusual and striking degree, all of the
qualities, or most of them, which most obviously distinguish the average man from the babboon. . . . The
chief of these qualities is a sort of restless impatience
with things as they are—a sort of insatiable desire to
help along the evolutionary process. The man who possesses this quality is ceaselessly eager to increase and
fortify his mastery of his environment. He has a vast
curiosity and a vast passion for solving the problems it
unrolls before him. . . .

---

[4] Reprinted from *Men vs. the Man,* with the permission of the publishers, Henry Holt and Company.

INTELLECTUAL REVOLT IN AMERICA
By *Harold E. Stearns* [5]

Thought is nourished by the soil it feeds on, and in America today that soil is choked with the feckless weeds of correctness. Our sanitary perfection, our material organization of goods, our muffling of emotion, our deprecation of curiosity, our fear of idle adventure, our horror of disease and death, our denial of suffering—what kind of soil of life is that?

Surely not an over-gracious or thrilling one; small wonder that our intellectual plants wither in this carefully aseptic sunlight.

Nevertheless, though I was tempted to give the subtitle "A Study in Sterility" to this essay, I do not believe that our soil is wholly sterile. Beneath the surface barrenness stirs a germinal energy that may yet push its way through the weeds and the tin cans of those who are afraid of life. If the genteel tradition did not succumb to the broad challenge of Whitman, his invitations have not been wholly rejected by the second generation following him. The most hopeful thing of intellectual promise in America today is the contempt of the younger people for their elders; they are restless, uneasy, disaffected. It is not a disciplined contempt; it is not yet kindled by any real love of intellectual values —how could it be? Yet it is a genuine and moving at-

[5] From his essay, "The Intellectual Life," in *Civilization in the United States,* by Thirty Americans. Reprinted here with the permission of the publishers, Harcourt, Brace and Company.

tempt to create a way of life free from the bondage of
an authority that has lost all meaning, even to those
who wield it. Some it drives in futile and pathetic ex-
patriotism from the country; others it makes head-
strong and reckless; many it forces underground, where,
much as in Russia before the revolution of 1905, the
intelligentsia meet their own kind and share the difficulties of their common struggle against an environment that is out to destroy them. But whatever its
crudeness and headiness, it is a yeast composed always
of those who *will not* conform. The more the pressure
of standardization is applied to them, the sharper and
keener—if often the wilder—becomes their rebellion
against it. . . .

The flashing beauty of form, the rising step of confident animalism, the quick smile of fertile minds—must
all these things, too, be reduced to a drab uniformity because we lack the courage to proclaim their sheer physical loveliness? Has not the magic of America been hidden under a fog of ugliness by those who never really
loved it, who never knew our natural gayety and high
spirits and eagerness for knowledge? They have the upper hand now—but who would dare to prophesy that
they can keep it?

Perhaps this is only a day-dream, but surely one can
hope that the America of our natural affections rather
than the present one of enforced dull standardization
may some day snap the shackles of those who today
keep it a spiritual prison. And as surely will it be the
rebellious and disaffected who accomplish the miracle, if

it is ever accomplished. Because at bottom their revolt, unlike the aggressions of the standardizers, is founded not on hate of what they cannot understand, but on love of what they wish all to share.

THE CONSERVATIVE [6]

By *Charles A. Bennett*

Charles A. Bennett is a professor of philosophy at Yale University. The selection is from his book of informal essays, *At a Venture*.

First he needs to be defined. Well, then . . . Tennyson once wrote in his sententious way:

> That man's the true Conservative
> Who lops the molder'd branch away.

No; I do not mean that. I prefer that definition given by some unknown epigrammatist, "A conservative is a man who believes that nothing should ever be done for the first time." That is perfect. It catches the essence of the man and his creed—the opposition to change not because it disturbs the existing order, but just because it is change; natural human inertia reflected upon and transformed into a philosophy—a fact turned into a theory to justify the fact.

Of course, he never states his philosophy in such simple, naked form; this is, so to speak, the main root or trunk which proliferates and burgeons into a matted tropical growth of subordinate dogmas and middle

[6] Reprinted with the permission of the author and of the publishers, Harper and Sons.

axioms. One may get instruction and entertainment from examining some of these.

There is, for example, the great and sacrosanct principle of Continuity. In explaining what this means he will inform you, with the air of one patiently bestowing enlightenment, that before the time of Darwin men believed in catastrophic change. Social transformations were revolutionary; in religious life sudden and violent conversion was popular; the course of nature was supposed to be subject to upheavals and miraculous interventions. But Darwin changed all that. Now we know that *natura non facit saltum*, and our motto must henceforward be, "Not revolution, but evolution." In practice the principle seems to come to this—that every change must be so slight, gradual, and inconspicuous as hardly to amount to a change at all. Any change, therefore, which is perceptible is for that very reason undesirable and is to be dismissed from consideration with the gnomic warning that it is no good trying to introduce Utopias overnight. We must confine ourselves to making infinitesimal alterations—that is, we must do practically nothing at a time; the inference being that if only every one will busy himself with effecting practically nothing at a time, in a million years or so Utopia will have been silently and almost automatically achieved.

Then there is the great principle of Compromise. It rests upon an axiom which runs: After all, we live in a practical world. It may be exhibited in a simple example. A wants to paint a wall black. B wants to paint it white. They finally agree to paint it gray. That is compromise. The peculiar virtue of this device is that, in time, A and B come to believe that, in a practical, rough-and-tumble world, gray—a nice, conservative gray, as the tailors have it—is the only possible color for walls. Any one who believes that walls either can or should be painted black or white or any color that is not strict gray, thereby declares himself an Extremist, a Crank, an Absolutist, an Idealist, a Doctrinaire, and an Unpractical Visionary. And once you have called a man by one of these names you need seek no further for epithets with which to discredit himself and his policy.

Passing over such notable principles as "You can't turn back the hands of the clock," "The best way to change a bad law is to obey it," "Don't swap horses when crossing the stream," "*Festina lente,*" and "Reform from within," I will mention only one other conservative formula. It is known as The Necessity for Looking on the Bright Side of Things. This is fundamental, for the desire for change starts from a perception of badness somewhere, and if you want to resist change you must be able to show that every item of bad is somehow counterbalanced by an item of good. From this we infer that it is as dangerous to tamper with this equilibrium as with the balance of nature. So, if some one calls your attention to intolerable industrial conditions, you maintain that this represents only one side of the picture, and that one could discover plenty of just employers and contented employees if one only looked for them. Or suppose you are offered the aggressive and repulsive mediocrity of *Main Street* as a true picture of life, you deny it hotly, averring that the author deliberately selected the unpleasant elements, and that he could have easily discerned many admirable and even lovable traits in his characters if he had taken the trouble to look for them. Obviously, then, there is no need to do anything about the industrial system or *Main Street*.

NOR YET THE NEW [7]

By Charles H. Grandgent

Professor Grandgent for many years has been head of the Romance Language Department of Harvard University. The essay from which the quotation below is made was given first as an address to the Smith College chapter of Phi Beta Kappa, in May, 1919. It now forms part of his book, *Old and New*.

Old things need not be therefore true,
O brother man, nor yet the new.

When Arthur Hugh Clough penned these lines, he little dreamed how quickly the second member of his apparently axiomatic proposition would become obsolete. "*New* things need not be therefore true"? It sounds like an echo from a forgotten past; yet only a few score years ago it was a perfectly safe assertion, as safe as "All's not gold that glitters," or "Where there's a will there's a way."

There was a time when the old had the right of way

[7] Reprinted with the permission of the author and of the publishers, the Harvard University Press.

and the new had to turn out or force its passage, when
the idea of innovation gave pause, when the successful
or even the unsuccessful experience of ages created a
presumption in favor of accepted usage, when a departure from tradition demanded an excuse. "I love
everything that's old," says one of the characters in *She
Stoops to Conquer,* "old friends, old times, old manners, old books, old wine." The same author once said:
"When I was a young man, being anxious to distinguish myself, I was perpetually starting new propositions. But I soon gave this over; for I found that generally what was new was false." Of well-nigh universal
application was the opinion uttered later by Daniel
Webster with reference to a certain political platform:
"What is valuable is not new, and what is new is not
valuable."

"We have changed all that," as Molière's quack doctor observed. The heart and the liver no longer abide in
the respective places to which the former school of med-
icine—and its accomplice, Dame Nature—assigned
them. "Time-honored custom" is without honor. The
very word "time-honored" is now used ordinarily in de-
rision. To say that a thing is old is to condemn it without a trial. An old style must be a bad one, an old
thought is not worth thinking. What we admire is the
"music of the future," the "new art," the "modern
school." To a strictly judicial mind, it would seem, the
quality of age or of novelty would carry no necessary
implication of value; the question of acceptance would
be decided on the basis of intrinsic merit. But the judi-

cial mind is rare. We are unconsciously swept along by the tide of opinion, and that tide has set in the direction of the untried. . . .

This brings me to the real subject of my discussion, the fashion of rebellion. For the insurgent attitude has now become a pose. With sundry ups and downs, the fortune of the Miltonic Satan has prospered, until in our generation he has become a favorite society figure. The drawing-room anarchist, the literary rebel, the artistic iconoclast, lay down the law for all of us. Among the conventions of the day, the most conspicuous is the convention of revolt. The only really unconventional person among us is the one who is not revolting against convention. If we wish to praise a young poet or painter, we must begin by making it plain that he is a revolter. Magazines, books, pictures are in full tilt against some invisible adversary; and one must be very old-fashioned, as well as very bold, to ask whether the mysterious foe can by any possibility be a windmill. Occasionally, however, an elderly swimmer does contrive to lift his head sufficiently out of the flood to wonder what it is all about.

A good many years ago there was in Boston a national assembly of Christian Endeavors. They swarmed in streets, shops, parks, eating-houses, one could scarcely stir without stepping on them; and their general aspect was that of holiday-makers. After conscientiously studying them for several days, an observer timidly inquired: "Are these people endeavoring to do anything in particular, or are they just endeavoring?" We might, if we dared, put a similar question to our revolters: "Are you revolting against anything in particular, or are you just revolting?" Many of them, I suspect, would be at a loss for an answer; after a moment's cogitation, however, they would doubtless reply that they were revolting against the Victorian Age. And, in fact, the Victorian Age appears to be the special butt of their scorn. In the rich vocabulary of their terms of obloquy, "Victorian" is the very worst. It designates self-complacency, cant, hypocrisy, convention—not the convention of revolt, of course, but the convention of decency. Quite vainly would one plead that the Age of Victoria, rated according to genius, bids fair to take rank with the ages of Pericles, Augustus, Elizabeth, and Louis XIV; that future generations may possibly regard the time of Thackeray, Dickens, George Eliot, George Meredith, Thomas Hardy, of Browning and Tennyson, of Arnold and Newman, of Mill and Darwin and Huxley and Spencer and Kelvin and Lister as rather a hard one to match in the annals of letters and science. Such a suggestion would, of course, appeal only to critics who knew the Victorian Age and some other ages. One might, however, put forward with more confidence the consideration that the Victorian Age has been dead for a good while, and that it is a pure waste of hind-leg power to go on forever kicking at a corpse. Still, even that argument would probably be unavailing; so stubborn is the corpse-kicking habit, so firmly rooted is convention. Indeed, if I mistake not, I have never come across a convention more hidebound than this same convention of revolt.

CONSOLATIONS OF THE CONSERVATIVE [8]

By Agnes Repplier

Among the essayists of the last half century, Miss Repplier holds a high place. Her writing is marked by charm and fine intelligence. The essay here quoted in part is from her book, *Points of Friction*.

There is a story of Hawthorne's which is little known, because it is too expansively dull to be read. It tells how the nations of the earth, convulsed by a mighty spasm of reform, rid themselves of the tools and symbols of all they held in abhorrence. Because they would have no more war, they destroyed the weapons of the world. Because they would have no more drunkenness, they destroyed its wines and spirits. Because they banned self-indulgence, they destroyed tobacco, tea, and coffee. Because they would have all men to be equal, they destroyed the insignia of rank, from the crown jewels of England to the medal of the Cincinnati. Wealth itself was not permitted to survive, lest the new order be as corrupt as was the old. Nothing was left but the human heart with its imperishable and inalienable qualities; and while it beats within the human breast, the world must still be molded by its passions. "When Cain wished to

[8] Reprinted with the permission of the publishers, the Houghton Mifflin Company.

slay his brother," murmured a cynic, watching the great guns trundled to the blaze, "he was at no loss for a weapon."

If belief in the perfectibility of man—and not of man only, but of governments—is the inspiration of liberalism, of radicalism, of the spirit that calls clamorously for change, and that has requisitioned the words reform and progression, sympathy with man and with his work, with the beautiful and imperfect things he has made of the checkered centuries, is the keynote of conservatism. The temperamental conservative is a type vulnerable to ridicule, yet not more innately ridiculous than his neighbors. He has been carelessly defined as a man who is cautious because he has a good income, and content because he is well placed; who is thick-headed because he lacks vision, and close-hearted because he is deaf to the moaning wind which is the cry of unhappy humanity asking justice from a world which has never known how to be just. Lecky, who had a neat hand at analysis, characterized the great conflicting parties in an axiom which pleased neither: "Stupidity in all its forms is Tory; folly in all its forms is Whig. . . ."

If we had resolutely severed the word "idealism" from the bloody chaos which is Russia, we should have understood more clearly, and have judged no less leniently, the seething ambitions of men who passionately desired, and desire, control. The elemental instinct of self-preservation is the first step to the equally elemental instinct of self-interest. Natural rights, about which we chatter freely, are not more equably preserved by deny-

ing them to one class of men than by denying them to
another. They have been ill protected under militarism
and capitalism, and their subversion has been a sin
crying out to Heaven for vengeance. They are not protected at all under any Soviet government so far known
to report.

Nothing is easier than to make the world safe for
democracy. Democracy is playing her own hand in the
game. She has every intention and every opportunity to
make the world safe for herself. But democracy may
be divorced from freedom, and freedom is the breath of
man's nostrils, the strength of his sinews, the sanction
of his soul. It is as painful to be tyrannized over by a
proletariat as by a tsar or by a corporation, and it is in
a measure more disconcerting, because of the greater in-
cohesion of the process. It is as revolting to be robbed
by a reformer as by a trust. Oppressive taxation, which
forced the great Revolution upon France; dishonest
"deals," which have made a mockery of justice in the
United States; ironic laws, framed for the convenient
looting of the bourgeoisie in Russia—there is as much
idealism in one device as in the others. Sonorous phrases
like "reconstruction of the world's psychology," and
"creation of a new world-atmosphere," are mental seda-
tives, drug-words, calculated to put to sleep any uneasy
apprehensions. They may mean anything, and they do
mean nothing, so that it is safe to go on repeating them.
But a Bolshevist official was arrested in Petrograd in
March, 1919, charged with embezzling fifteen million
rubles. Not content with the excesses of the new régime,

he must needs revert to the excesses of the old—a dis-
couraging study in evolution.

DRIFT [9]

By Walter Lippmann

It seems as if the most obvious way of reacting toward
evil were to consider it a lapse from grace. The New
Freedom, we are told, is "only the old revived and
clothed in the unconquerable strength of modern America." Everywhere you hear it: that the people have been
"deprived" of ancient rights, and legislation is framed
on the notion that we can recover the alleged democracy
of early America.

I once read in a learned magazine an essay on "The
Obliviscence of the Disagreeable." As I remember it,
the writer was trying to demonstrate what he regarded
as a very hopeful truth—that men tend to forget pain
more easily than pleasure. That is no doubt a comfort-
able faculty, but it plays havoc with history. For in
regard to those early days of the Republic, most of our
notions are marked by a well-nigh total obliviscence of
the disagreeable. We find it very difficult to remember
that there were sharp class divisions in the young Republic, that suffrage was severely restricted, that the
Fathers were a very conscious upper class determined to
maintain their privileges. Nations make their histories
to fit their illusions. That is why reformers are so anx-

[9] Reprinted from *Drift and Mastery*, by permission of and arrangement
with the publishers, Henry Holt and Company.

ious to return to early America. What they know of it comes to them filtered through the golden lies of school-books and hallowed by the generous loyalty of their childhood.

Men generally find in the past what they miss in the present. During the Paterson strike of 1913, I heard a very drastic I. W. W. agitator tell a meeting of silk-weavers that they had fallen low since the days of the great Chief Justice Marshall. In those days there were no rich and poor, and the Constitution had not yet been abrogated by an impudent Chief of Police! Yet in the days of Marshall even the most peaceful trade union was outlawed, and as for the doctrines of the I. W. W.— imagine the sentiments of Alexander Hamilton. A few years ago I was living in Boston when an old gentleman, unhappy over the trend of democracy, published a book to glorify the American Tories. It consisted largely of intimate details from the private lives of the revolutionary heroes. Boston wouldn't have the book, true or untrue. So the old gentleman was denounced and his book forgotten.

For most of us insist that somewhere in the past there was a golden age. The modern puritan locates it in the period of the most famous ancestors from whom he can claim descent. That ancestor regretted the loss of Eden. Rousseau's millennial dream was a "state of nature." Hard-headed Adam Smith had his "original state" which was all that England wasn't. I know literary men who lament the passing of the eighteenth-century coffee house, and New York is full of artists who dream of Parisian cafés. Zionists go back to David and Solomon; Celtic revivalists worry about Kathleen ni Houlihan; Chesterton dreams of Merrie England; scholars yearn for fifth-century Athens; there is a considerable vogue today for certain of the earlier Egyptian dynasties, and some people, more radical than others, regard civilization itself as a disease.

The prototype of all revivals is each man's wistful sense of his own childhood. There is something infinitely pathetic in the way we persist in recalling what is by its very nature irrevocable. Perhaps each of us is touched by unuttered disappointments, and life has not the taste we anticipated. The weary man sinks back into the past, like a frightened child into its mother's arms. He glorifies what is gone when he fears what is to come. That is why discontented husbands have a way of admiring the cakes that mother used to bake. Beaten nations live in the exploits of their ancestors, and all exiles lament by the waters of Babylon. The curse of Ireland, of Poland, of Alsace is that they cannot forget what they were. There are no people who cling so ardently to a family tree as do those who have come down in the world. The men who were beaten by the trusts will never see the promise of the trusts.

Whenever the future is menacing and unfamiliar, whenever the day's work seems insurmountable, men seek some comfort in the warmth of memory. Only those who are really at home in their world find life more interesting as they mature. Experience for them is not an awful chance, but a prize they can win and embrace. They need no romance to make life tolerable. But people who are forever dreaming of a mythical past are merely saying that they are afraid of the future. They will falter before their problems, will deal with them half-heartedly and with diffidence. Their allegiance is not to the world. And they will never give themselves entirely to the task of making for themselves on this earth and in their age an adequate and civilized home.

The past which men create for themselves is a place where thought is unnecessary and happiness inevitable. The American temperament leans generally to a kind of mystical anarchism, in which the "natural" humanity in each man is adored as the savior of society. You meet this faith throughout the thousand and one communistic experiments and new religions in which America is so abundant. "If only you let men alone, they'll be good," a typical American reformer said to me the other day. He believed, as most Americans do, in the unsophisticated man, in his basic kindliness and his instinctive practical sense. A critical outlook seemed to the reformer an inhuman one; he distrusted, as Bryan does, the appearance of the expert; he believed that whatever faults the common man might show were due to some kind of Machiavellian corruption.

He had the American dream, which may be summed up, I think, in the statement that the undisciplined man is the salt of the earth. So when the trusts appeared, when the free land was gone, and America had been congested into a nation, the only philosophy with any weight of tradition behind it was a belief in the virtues of the spontaneous, enterprising, untrained, and unsocialized man. Trust promoters cried: Let us alone. The little business men cried: We're the natural men; so let us alone. And the public cried: We're the most natural of all; so please do stop interfering with us. Muck-raking gave an utterance to the small business men and to the larger public, who dominated reform politics. What did they do? They tried by all the machinery and power they could muster to restore a business world in which each man could again be left to his own will—a world that needed no coöperative intelligence. In the Sherman Act is symbolized this deliberate attempt to recreate an undeliberate society. No group of people, except the socialists, wished to take up the enormous task of disciplining business to popular need. For the real American was dreaming of the Golden Age in which he could drift with impunity.

But there has arisen in our time a large group of people who look to the future. They talk a great deal about their ultimate goal. Many of them do not differ in any essential way from those who dream of a glorious past. They put Paradise before them instead of behind them. They are going to be so rich, so great, and so happy some day, that any concern about tomorrow seems a bit sordid. They didn't fall from Heaven, as the reactionaries say, but they are going to Heaven with the radicals. Now this habit of reposing in the sun of a brilliant future is very enervating. It opens a chasm between fact and fancy, and the whole fine dream is detached from the living zone of the present. At the only point where effort and intelligence are needed, that point where today is turning into tomorrow, there these people are not found. At the point where human direction counts most they do not direct. So they are like most anarchists, wild in their dreams and unimportant in their deeds. They cultivate a castle in Spain and a flat in Harlem; a princess in the air and a drudge in the kitchen.

Then, too, there are the darlings of evolution. They are quite certain that evolution, as they put it, is ever onward and upward. For them all things conspire to achieve that well-known, though unmentioned far-off divine event to which the whole creation moves. They seem to imply as Moody suggested:

"I, I, last product of the toiling ages,
    Goal of heroic feet that never lagged—"

though

"A little thing in trousers, slightly jagged."

How the conservative goes to work with the idea of evolution has been ably exposed by William English Walling. First, assume "progress" by calling it inevitable: this obviates the necessity for any practical change just now. Then assert the indubitable fact that real progress is very slow: and infer that wisdom consists in deprecating haste. Now when you have called progress inevitable and imperceptible, you have done about all that philosophy could do to justify impotence.

The radical view of evolution is more optimistic, but not more intelligent. In fact, it is generally all optimism and little else. For though it doesn't quite dare to say that whatever is, is right, it does assume that whatever is going to be, is going to be right. I believe that G. K. Chesterton once called this sort of thing progressivism by the calendar. There is complete confidence that whatever is later in time is better in fact, that the next phase is the desirable one, that all change is "upward," that God and Nature are collaborating in our blithe ascent to the Superman. Such an outlook undermines judgment and initiative, deliberate effort, invention, plan, and sets you adrift on the currents of time, hoping for impossible harbors.

In a constructive social movement the harm done is immeasurable. The most vivid illustration is that of the old-fashioned, fatalistic Marxian socialists. They have an implicit faith that human destiny is merely the unfolding of an original plan, some of the sketches of which are in their possession, thanks to the labors of Karl Marx. Strictly speaking, these men are not revolutionists as they believe themselves to be; they are the interested pedants of destiny. They are God's audience, and they know the plot so well that occasionally they prompt Him. In their system all that education, unions, leadership, and thought can do is to push along what by the theory needs no pushing. These socialists are like the clown Marceline at the Hippodrome, who was always very busy assisting in labor that would be done whether he were there or not. They face the ancient dilemma of fatalism: whatever they do is right, and nothing they do matters. Go to almost any socialist meeting and you'll hear it said that socialism would come if the Socialist Party had never been heard from. Perhaps so. But why organize a Socialist Party?

Of course, socialists don't act upon their theory. They are too deeply impressed with the evil that exists, too eager for the future that they see, to trust entirely in the logic of events. They do try to shape that future. But their old fatalism hampers them enormously the moment any kind of action is proposed. They are out of sympathy with conservative trade unionism, but they are still more hostile to the I. W. W. In politics they despise the reformer, but when they themselves obtain office they do nothing that a hundred "bourgeois" reformers haven't done before them. The Socialist Party in this country has failed to develop a practical program for labor or a practical program for politics. It claims to have a different philosophy from that of trade unionists or reformers, but when you try to judge the difference by its concrete results, it is imperceptible.

The theory and the temper of orthodox socialism are fatalistic, and no fatalist can really give advice. Theory and practice are widely sundered in the American socialist movement. There is a stumbling revolt which lives from hand to mouth, a catch-as-catch-can struggle, and then far removed from it, standing in majesty, a great citadel of dogma almost impervious to new ideas. For in the real world, destiny is one of the aliases of drift.

Closely related in essence, though outwardly quite different, is what might be called the panacea habit of mind. Beginning very often in some penetrating insight or successful analysis, this sort of mind soon becomes incapable of seeing anything besides that portion of reality which sustains the insight and is subject to the analysis. A good idea, in short, becomes a fixed idea. One group of American socialists can see only the advantage of strikes, another of ballots. One reformer sees the advantages of the direct primaries in Wisconsin: they become the universal solvent of political evil. You find engineers who don't see why you can't build society on the analogy of a steam engine; you find lawyers, like Taft, who see in the courts an intimation of Heaven; sanitation experts who wish to treat the whole world as one vast sanitarium; lovers who wish to treat it as one vast happy family; education enthusiasts who wish to treat it as one vast nursery. No one who undertook to be the Balzac of reform by writing its Human Comedy could afford to miss the way in which the reformer in each profession tends to make his specialty an analogy for the whole of life. The most amazing of all are people who deal with the currency question. Somehow or other, long meditation seems to produce in them a feeling that they are dealing with the crux of human difficulties.

Then there is the panacea most frequently propounded by voluble millionaires: the high cost of living is the cost of high living, and thrift is the queen of the virtues. Sobriety is another virtue, highly commended—

in fact there are thousands of people who seriously regard it as the supreme social virtue. To those of us who are sober and still discontented, the effort to found a political party on a colossal *Don't* is not very inspiring. After thrift and sobriety, there is always efficiency, a word which covers a multitude of confusions. No one in his senses denies the importance of efficient action, just as no one denies thrift and sober living. It is only when these virtues become the prime duty of man that we rejoice in the poet who has the courage to glorify the vagabond, preach a saving indolence, and glorify Dionysus. Be not righteous overmuch is merely a terse way of saying that virtue can defeat its own ends. Certainly, whenever a negative command like sobriety absorbs too much attention, and morality is obstinate and awkward, then living men have become cluttered in what was meant to serve them.

There are thousands today who, out of patience with almost everything, believe passionately that some one change will set everything right. In the first rank stand the suffragettes who believe that votes for women will make men chaste. I have just read a book by a college professor which announces that the short ballot will be as deep a revolution as the abolition of slavery. There are innumerable Americans who believe that a democratic constitution would create a democracy. Of course, there are single taxers so single-minded that they believe a happy civilization would result from the socialization of land values. Everything else that seems to be needed would follow spontaneously if only the land monopoly were abolished.

The syndicalists suffer from this habit of mind in an acute form. They refuse to consider any scheme for the reorganization of industry. All that will follow, they say, if only you can produce a General Strike. But obviously you might paralyze society, you might make the proletariat supreme, and still leave the proletariat without the slightest idea of what to do with the power it had won.

What happens is that men gain some insight into society and concentrate their energy upon it. Then when the facts rise up in their relentless complexity, the only way to escape them is to say: Never mind; do what I advocate, and all these other things shall be added unto you.

There is still another way of reacting toward a too complicated world. That way is to see so much good in every reform that you can't make up your mind where to apply your own magnificent talents. The result is that you don't apply your talents at all.

Reform produces its Don Quixotes who never deal with reality; it produces its Brands who are single-minded to the brink of ruin; and it produces its Hamlets and its Rudins who can never make up their minds. What is common to them all is a failure to deal with the real world in the light of its possibilities. To try to follow all the aliases of drift is like attacking the hydra by cutting off its heads. The few examples given here of how men shirk self-government might be extended indefinitely. They are as common to radicals as to conservatives. You can find them flourishing in an orthodox church and among the most rebellious socialists.

Men will do almost anything but govern themselves. They don't want the responsibility. In the main, they are looking for some benevolent guardian, be it a "good man in office," or a perfect constitution, or the evolution of nature. They want to be taken in charge. If they have to think for themselves they turn either to the past or to a distant future: but they manage to escape the real effort of the imagination, which is to weave a dream into the turning present. They trust to destiny, a quick one or a slow one, and the whole task of judging events is avoided. They turn to automatic devices: human initiative can be ignored. They forbid evil, and then they feel better. They settle on a particular analogy, or a particular virtue, or a particular policy, and trust to luck that everything else will take care of itself.

But no one of these substitutes for self-government is really satisfactory, and the result is that a state of chronic rebellion appears. That is our present situation. The most hopeful thing about it is that through the confusion we can come to some closer understanding of why the modern man lacks stability, why his soul is scattered. We may, perhaps, be able to see a little better just what self-government implies.

The chronic rebellion is evident enough. I have a friend who after the Lawrence strike was a great admirer of the I. W. W. He told me about it one day

with tears in his eyes. Two months later I met him, and
he was cursing: "They're so successful that they're getting ready to throw So-and-So out of the I. W. W. for
heresy." It is one of the ironies of the labor movement
that it preaches solidarity, and seems to propagate by
fission. For there is large truth in the saying that the
only thing anarchists hate more than tyrants is an
anarchist who differs with them. Indeed the bitterness
between the "red" and the "yellow" unions is at least
as great as the bitterness between the unions and the
employers. The I. W. W. hates the American Federation
of Labor and many political socialists with a vindictive-
ness that makes no distinction between them and the
most tyrannical boss. Revolt within the world of revolt
is an institution. If any capitalist thinks he is the object
of abuse, he ought to come and hear a debate between
the Detroit I. W. W. and the Chicago I. W. W., between believers in "direct" and in "political" action,
between "State Socialists" and Syndicalists.

The sects of the rebellious are like the variety of the
Protestant churches, and they are due to a similar
cause. Once the churches had cut off from the deeply-
rooted central tradition of Rome, they continued to
cut off from each other. Now Protestantism was an
effort at a little democracy in religion, and its history is
amazingly like that of all the other revolts from the old
absolutisms. For once men had broken loose from the
cohesion and obedience of the older life, the floundering
of democracy began. It was not so easy to become self-
governing as it was to bowl over a tyrant. And the long

history of schisms is really the story of how men set up a substitute for authority, and had to revolt against it. To a man standing on the firm foundation of an ancient faith, the instability of self-government is its just punishment, and no doubt he smiles at the folly of men who give up security and peace for a mess of revolt.

After Protestantism, the Romantic movement and the birth of political democracy. It is hardly necessary to recall what troubled spirits the romanticists were, how terrible the disillusionments. Their histories were with few exceptions tragic: and the "unending pursuit of the ever-fleeting object of desire" led many of them back into the arms of the Catholic Church. One has only to read the lives of the men whose names stand out in the nineteenth century to realize that the epoch of revolt produced tortured and driven spirits. Whatever their virtues, and they are many, they never attained that inner harmony whose outward sign is a cordial human life.

No one has felt this more poignantly than the modern artist. Lost in the clamor of commercialism, many painters seem to insist that if they can't make themselves admired they will at least make themselves heard. And of course, if you live in a world of studios, drawing-rooms, and cafés, amidst idle people in little cliques, you have to draw attention to yourself from the outside world in some other way than by decorating or interpreting human life. The modern artist can secure attention, but he can't hold it. For the world is so complex that he can't find common experiences and common aspirations to deal with. And because he can't do this, he can't become artist to a nation. He has to be satisfied with a cult. So he specializes on some aspect of form, exaggerates some quality of line, and produces art that only a few people would miss if it disappeared. Then he denounces the philistine public.

But in his heart he is unsatisfied with his work, and so he too develops a habit of chronic rebellion: a school is no sooner founded than there is a secession. The usual manifesto is published (they all say about the same thing): authority and classicism are denounced in the name of youth and adventure. "All I want," said a friend of mine who paints, "is to bewilder and fascinate. . . ." "All we need is wiggle," said another. "To be alive is to rebel," said a third. But I venture to suggest that what the rebels are rebelling against is not a classical authority: none exists today that has any compelling force. They are in rebellion against something within themselves; there are conflicts in their souls for which they have found no solution; and their revolt is the endless pursuit of what their own disharmony will never let them find.

"Nor certitude, nor peace, nor help for pain;
 And we are here as on a darkling plain
 Swept with confused alarms of struggle and flight,
 Where ignorant armies clash by night."

This certitude for which Matthew Arnold cries, where has it gone?

Classicists, like Professor Babbitt of Harvard, or Mr.

Paul Elmer More, say that it has gone with the shattering of external authority in the *débâcle* of Romanticism and the French Revolution. Their remedy for the chaos and ineptitude of modern life is a return to what they describe as eternal forms of justice and moderation. They would revive authority with its dominating critics like Boileau. Romanticism for them is a lapse from grace, full of sweet sin, and they hope to return to the Golden Age of the classics.

I don't see how this dream can succeed. Their solution is built on a wild impossibility, for in order to realize it they will have to abolish machinery and communication, newspapers and popular books. They will have to call upon some fairy to wipe out the memory of the last hundred years, and they will have to find a magician who can conjure up a church and monarchy that men will obey. They can't do any of these things, though they can bewail the fact and display their grief by unremitting hostility to the modern world.

But though their remedy is, I believe, altogether academic, their diagnosis does locate the spiritual problem. We have lost authority. We are "emancipated" from an ordered world. We drift.

The loss of something outside ourselves which we can obey is a revolutionary break with our habits. Never before have we had to rely so completely upon ourselves. No guardian to think for us, no precedent to follow without question, no lawmaker above, only ordinary men set to deal with heart-breaking perplexity. All weakness comes to the surface. We are homeless in a jungle of machines and untamed powers that haunt and lure the imagination. Of course, our culture is confused, our thinking spasmodic, and our emotion out of kilter. No mariner ever enters upon a more uncharted sea than does the average human being born into the twentieth century. Our ancestors thought they knew their way from birth through all eternity: we are puzzled about the day after tomorrow.

What nonsense it is, then, to talk of liberty as if it were a happy-go-lucky breaking of chains. It is with emancipation that real tasks begin, and liberty is a searching challenge, for it takes away the guardianship of the master and the comfort of the priest. The iconoclasts didn't free us. They threw us into the water, and now we have to swim.

THE MENACE OF THE MACHINE [10]
By André Siegfried

M. Siegfried is a French scholar in the field of economics, and for some years has been attached to the French foreign office as an economic expert. He has taken part in the various meetings of the League of Nations. Post-war conditions in America have been a subject of particular study with him, and he has been called "the keenest critic that America has known in fifty years." The passage quoted below constitutes the last chapter of his recent book, *America Comes of Age*.

The America that Columbus discovered was to our ancestors geographically a new world. Today, as a result of the revolutionary changes brought about by

[10] Reprinted with the permission of Harcourt, Brace and Company.

modern methods of production, it has again become a new world, and furthermore we have still to rediscover it.

Having first cleared away all hampering traditions and political obstacles, the American people are now creating on a vast scale an entirely original social structure which bears only a superficial resemblance to the European. It may even be a new age, an age in which Europe is to be relegated to a niche in the history of mankind; for Europe is no longer the driving force of the world. The old European civilization did not really cross the Atlantic, for the American reawakening is not, as is generally supposed, simply a matter of degrees and dimensions; it is the creation of new conceptions. Many of the most magnificent material achievements of the United States have been made possible only by sacrificing certain rights of the individual, rights which we in the Old World regard as among the most precious victories of civilization. In spite of their identical religious and ethnic origin, Europe and America are diverging in their respective scales of value. This contrast was brought to a head by the war, which installed the United States prematurely in an unassailable position of economic supremacy. To America the advent of the new order is a cause for pride, but to Europe it brings heart-burnings and regrets for a state of society that is doomed to disappear.

From an economic point of view, America is sane and healthy. Her prosperity in spite of possible setbacks rests on her vast natural resources and on the unexcelled efficiency of her means of production. Thanks to the abundance of her raw materials, her conquest of wealth has reached a point unknown elsewhere. To the American, Europe is a land of paupers, and Asia a continent of starving wretches. Luxury in every-day consumption and the extension to the many living conditions previously reserved for the few—these are new phenomena in the history of mankind, and are undoubtedly evidence of splendid progress. But what is absolutely new about this society which is accomplishing such marvels is that in all its many aspects—even including idealism and religion—it is working toward the single goal of production. It is a materialistic society, organized to produce things rather than people, with output set up as a god. Never before in history have social forces converged on so vast and so intensive a scale, but even the extent of the created wealth is less remarkable than the dynamic force of the human impulse that has brought this wealth into being.

Europe squanders her man-power and spares her substance, but America does exactly the reverse. For the past half-century, and especially during the last ten years, the Americans have been concentrating on the problem of obtaining the maximum efficiency of each worker. As a result of the use of machinery, of standardization, and of intensive division and organization of labor, productive methods have been renovated to a degree that few Europeans have ever dreamed of. In this super-collectivism, however, lies grave risk for the individual. His integrity is seriously threatened not only as a producer, but as a consumer as well.

If the aim of society is to produce the greatest amount of comfort and luxury for the greatest number of people, then the United States of America is in a fair way to succeed. And yet a house, a bath, and a car for every workman—so much luxury within the reach of all —can only be obtained at a tragic price, no less than the transformation of millions of workmen into automatons. "Fordism," which is the essence of American industry, results in the standardization of the workman himself. Artisanship, now out of date, has no place in the New World, but with it have disappeared certain conceptions of mankind which we in Europe consider the very basis of civilization. To express his own personality through his creative efforts is the ambition of every Frenchman, but it is incompatible with mass production.

We must not imagine that thoughtful Americans are unaware of the peril which is threatening their manhood, but it is too much to expect them to sacrifice their machines; for they give production priority over everything else. Having refused to save the individuality of the factory worker, they shift their defense to other grounds. During the day the worker may only be a cog in the machine, they say; but in the evening at any rate he becomes a man once more. His leisure, his money, the very things which mass production puts at his disposal, these will restore to him the manhood and intellectual independence of which his highly organized work has deprived him. This change in the center of gravity in the life of the individual marks an absolute revolution in the ideas on which society in Western Europe has been built up. Can it be possible that the personality of the individual can recover itself in consumption after being so crippled and weakened in production? Have not the very products, in the form in which they are turned out by the modern factory, lost their individuality as well?

One of the finest attainments of American democracy has been to give much the same things to her poorest and richest citizens alike. The banker has his Rolls-Royce and the workman has his Ford. The banker's wife has her Paquin gown, and the working-girl chooses a similar one from the enormous quantities produced after the minimum of delay. The same applies all through the list. This generalized comfort is possible, first, because production is concentrated on a limited number of models repeated *ad infinitum,* and secondly, because the public is willing to put up with it. Thus we are forced to conclude that the price that America pays for her undeniable material progress is the sacrifice of one aspect of civilization.

Thus they are advancing in one direction and retrogressing in another. The material advance is immeasurable in comparison with the Old World, but from the point of view of individual refinement and art, the sacrifice is real indeed. Even the humblest European sees in art an aristocratic symbol of his own personality, and modern America has no national art and does not even feel the need of one.

Once it is admitted that their conception of society is materialistic in spite of the idealism of its leaders, it is only logical that the doctrine of efficiency should become the central idea of the country. Today in America no sacrifice is too great to be endured for this sacred principle. There is no possible escape. Big profits overshadow liberty in all its forms, and the exercise of intelligence is encouraged only if it fits in with this common aim. Any one who turns aside to dabble in research or dilettantism is regarded as almost mentally perverted. Hence a growing tendency to reduce all virtues to the primordial ideal of conformity.

This point of view is not imposed by the upper classes or the government, but by the great masses of the people themselves. In the universities the majority of students are satisfied if they memorize an array of ready-made facts, and they seek from their professors not culture but the fundamentals of a successful career. In nothing does America more resemble Germany than in this discipline of thought. It may lead to splendid material results, and it is undoubtedly a marvelous aid to economic achievement; but under it originality and individual talent, and often art and genius, rebel or are stifled. France has the same instinctive fear of American methods as symbolized by Ford as she had of the German system on the eve of the War. Although she fully realizes that by the triumph of these methods the productivity of the world will increase tremendously, that things which now lie latent in our grasp, restricted and materially sterile, will blossom anew in the conquest of wealth, yet she hesitates to pay the price. She recalls with the force of a warning the quotation from Lucretius: *Propter vitam vitae perdere causas.*

An important transformation of society results from this concentration of energy on the one supreme object of mass production. The individual, having become a means rather than an end, accepts his *rôle* of cog in the immense machine without giving a passing thought to the effect on his personality. Religion, also enrolled in the movement, exalts production as an ideal akin to the mysticism of life and of human progress. The ideal of "service" sanctifies this collaboration and its superb material rewards. Caught between the atrophied individual and the over-disciplined community, the family finds its field of action greatly restricted; for in the eyes of the apostles of efficiency, the family is regarded as a barrier impeding the current. Though the Catholic Church still defends it, believing it to be one of its strongholds, yet society as a whole no longer relies on the home for the early training of the nation. It is to the public schools, the churches, to the ten thousand Y.M.C.A.'s and other associations for education and reform, to the press, and even to publicity that they look instead for the education of the masses. They pay little heed to the need of preserving for the jaded individual either the refuge of the family circle or the relaxation of meditation and culture. On the contrary, they consider them as obstacles in the way of progress. In the absence of an intermediate type of social institution in which co-operation is moderated by freedom, American society tends to adopt an aspect of practical collectivism. This collectivism is approved of by the upper classes and is whole-heartedly accepted by the masses; but it is subtly undermining the liberty of the individual and restricting his outlook to such an extent that without so much as regretting or realizing it, he himself assents to his own abnegation. In this respect the American community is closer to the ancient civilizations in which the individual belonged to the city-state than is the social fabric of Western Europe which has evolved from the Middle Ages and the French Revolution. The dreams of Rousseau have at length been realized, but not by the methods or under the conditions that he imagined, but strange to relate by a régime of industrialism that he could not possibly have foreseen.

Those who seem to suffer most under this discipline are the foreign-born of the upper classes, but certain mature Americans also protest against it. The youth of the country makes no objection, and there is no reaction of the individual against this moral tyranny. The nation is not individualistic in mentality, and it therefore accepts this collectivism as part of itself; and the régime really suits it. The material advantages are so great, the security so perfect, and the enthusiasm of collective action in accomplishing stupendous tasks so overwhelming, that in an almost mystical abandon, other considerations are neither heeded nor missed.

But can the individual possibly survive in such an

atmosphere? In her enthusiasm to perfect her material success, has not America risked quenching the flame of individual liberty which Europe has always regarded as one of the chief treasures of civilization? At the very moment that America is enjoying a state of prosperity such as the world has never known before, an impartial observer is forced to ask whether this unprecedented abundance of wealth will in the long run lead to a higher form of civilization. Europe, where industrial mass production was initiated, hesitates, terrified by the logical consequences. Will she end by adopting them? On the contrary, are they not incompatible with the old-established civilization which so expresses her personality? Some who are eager to rejuvenate industrial Europe look to America for inspiration and guidance; but others hold back, deeming the past superior and preferable.

When we visit America, we see Europe from a new perspective. It seems different from what we had imagined, and very different from the impression gained from the reproaches of Oriental thinkers. In the light of the American contrast we see that material pursuits have not entirely absorbed the soul of Europe, and that it can still appreciate free and disinterested thought and spiritual joys which can often be obtained only by renouncing comforts and fortune.

The chief contrast between Europe and America is not so much one of geography as a fundamental difference between two epochs in the history of mankind, each with its own conception of life. We have the contrast between industrial mass production which absorbs the individual for its material conquests, as against the individual considered not merely as a means of production and progress but as an independent ego. From this unusual aspect we perceive certain traits that are common to the psychology of both Europe and the Orient. So the discussion broadens until it becomes a dialogue, as it were, between Ford and Ghandi.

THE TEMPLE OF THE MIND [11]
By Bertrand Russell

Bertrand Russell is one of the ablest thinkers and writers in the liberal group in England. He has a brilliant and stimulating mind, and is fearless in the expression of his ideas. The following excerpt is taken from his essay, "A Free Man's Worship," in his book *Mysticism and Logic*. The student will notice that the first paragraph was quoted by Dean Inge in his essay on "The Idea of Progress."

That Man is the product of causes which had no prevision of the end they were achieving; that his origin, his growth, his hopes and fears, his loves and his beliefs, are but the outcome of accidental collocations of atoms; that no fire, no heroism, no intensity of thought and feeling, can preserve an individual life beyond the grave; that all the labors of the ages, all the devotion, all the inspiration, all the noonday brightness of human genius, are destined to extinction in the vast death of the solar system, and that the whole temple of Man's

[11] Reprinted by permission of and arrangement with the publishers, Longmans, Green, and Company.

achievement must inevitably be buried beneath the
débris of a universe in ruins—all these things, if not
quite beyond dispute, are yet so nearly certain, that no
philosophy which rejects them can hope to stand. Only
within the scaffolding of these truths, only on the firm
foundation of unyielding despair, can the soul's habitation henceforth be safely built.

How, in such an alien and inhuman world, can so
powerless a creature as Man preserve his aspirations un-
tarnished? A strange mystery it is that Nature, omnipotent but blind, in the revolutions of her secular hurry-
ings through the abysses of space, has brought forth at
last a child, subject still to her power, but gifted with
sight, with knowledge of good and evil, with the capacity of judging all the works of his unthinking
Mother. In spite of Death, the mark and seal of the
parental control, Man is yet free, during his brief years,
to examine, to criticize, to know, and in imagination to
create. To him alone, in the world with which he is
acquainted, this freedom belongs; and in this lies his
superiority to the resistless forces that control his outward life. . . .

To every man comes, sooner or later, the great renunciation. For the young, there is nothing unattainable;
a good thing desired with the whole force of a passionate
will, and yet impossible, is to them not credible. Yet, by
death, by illness, by poverty, or by the voice of duty,
we must learn, each one of us, that the world was not
made for us, and that, however beautiful may be the
things we crave, Fate may nevertheless forbid them. It

is the part of courage, when misfortune comes, to bear without repining the ruin of our hopes, to turn away our thoughts from vain regrets. This degree of submission to Power is not only just and right: it is the very gate of wisdom.

But passive renunciation is not the whole of wisdom; for not by renunciation alone can we build a temple for the worship of our own ideals. Haunting foreshadowings of the temple appear in the realm of imagination, in music, in architecture, in the untroubled kingdom of reason, and in the golden sunset magic of lyrics, where beauty shines and glows, remote from the touch of sorrow, remote from the fear of change, remote from the failures and disenchantments of the world of fact. In the contemplation of these things the vision of heaven will shape itself in our hearts, giving at once a touchstone to judge the world about us, and an inspiration by which to fashion to our needs whatever is not incapable of serving as a stone in the sacred temple. . . .

But the beauty of Tragedy does but make visible a quality which, in more or less obvious shapes, is present always and everywhere in life. In the spectacle of Death, in the endurance of intolerable pain, and in the irrevocableness of a vanished past, there is a sacredness, an overpowering awe, a feeling of the vastness, the depth, the inexhaustible mystery of existence, in which, as by some strange marriage of pain, the sufferer is bound to the world by bonds of sorrow. In these moments of insight, we lose all eagerness of temporary desire, all struggling and striving for petty ends, all care for the little trivial things that, to a superficial view, make up the common life of day by day; we see, surrounding the narrow raft illumined by the flickering light of human comradeship, the dark ocean on whose rolling waves we toss for a brief hour; from the great night without, a chill blast breaks in upon our refuge; all the loneliness of humanity amid hostile forces is concentrated upon the individual soul, which must struggle alone, with what of courage it can command, against the whole weight of a universe that cares nothing for its hopes and fears. Victory, in this struggle with the powers of darkness, is the true baptism into the glorious company of heroes, the true initiation into the overmastering beauty of human existence. From that awful encounter of the soul with the outer world, renunciation, wisdom, and charity are born; and with their birth a new life begins. To take into the inmost shrine of the soul the irresistible forces whose puppets we seem to be—Death and change, the irrevocableness of the past, and the powerlessness of man before the blind hurry of the universe from the vanity to vanity—to feel these things and know them is to conquer them.

This is the reason why the Past has such magical power. The beauty of its motionless and silent pictures is like the enchanted purity of late autumn, when the leaves, though one breath would make them fall, still glow against the sky in golden glory. The Past does not change or strive; like Duncan, after life's fitful fever it sleeps well; what was eager and grasping, what was

petty and transitory, has faded away, the things that
were beautiful and eternal shine out of it like stars in
the night. Its beauty, to a soul not worthy of it, is un-
endurable; but to a soul which has conquered Fate it
is the key of religion.

The life of Man, viewed outwardly, is but a small
thing in comparison with the forces of Nature. The
slave is doomed to worship Time and Fate and Death,
because they are greater than anything he finds in himself, and because all his thoughts are of things which
they devour. But, great as they are, to think of them
greatly, to feel their passionless splendor, is greater still.
And such thought makes us free men; we no longer
bow before the inevitable in Oriental subjection, but
we absorb it, and make it a part of ourselves. To abandon the struggle for private happiness, to expel all
eagerness of temporary desire, to burn with passion for
eternal things—this is emancipation, and this is the
free man's worship. And this liberation is effected by a
contemplation of Fate; for Fate itself is subdued by the
mind which leaves nothing to be purged by the purify-
ing fire of Time.

United with his fellow men by the strongest of all
ties, the tie of a common doom, the free man finds that
a new vision is with him always, shedding over every
daily task the light of love. The life of Man is a long
march through the night, surrounded by invisible foes,
tortured by weariness and pain, toward a goal that few
can hope to reach, and where none may tarry long. One
by one, as they march, our comrades vanish from our

sight, seized by the silent orders of omnipotent Death. Very brief is the time in which we can help them, in which their happiness or misery is decided. Be it ours to shed sunshine on their path, to lighten their sorrows by the balm of sympathy, to give them the pure joy of a never-tiring affection, to strengthen failing courage, to instill faith in hours of despair. Let us not weigh in grudging scales their merits and demerits, but let us think only of their need—of the sorrows, the difficulties, perhaps the blindnesses, that make the misery of their lives; let us remember that they are fellow sufferers in the same darkness, actors in the same tragedy with ourselves. And so, when their day is over, when their good and their evil have become eternal by the immortality of the past, be it ours to feel that, where they suffered, where they failed, no deed of ours was the cause; but wherever a spark of the divine fire kindled in their hearts, we were ready with encouragement, with sympathy, with brave words in which high courage glowed.

Brief and powerless is Man's life; on him and all his race the slow, sure doom falls pitiless and dark. Blind to good and evil, reckless of destruction, omnipotent matter rolls on its relentless way; for Man, condemned today to lose his dearest, tomorrow himself to pass through the gate of darkness, it remains only to cherish, ere yet the blow falls, the lofty thoughts that ennoble his little day; disdaining the coward terrors of the slave of Fate, to worship at the shrine that his own hands have built; undismayed by the empire of chance, to preserve a mind free from the wanton tyranny that rules his outward life; proudly defiant of the irresistible forces that tolerate, for a moment, his knowledge and his condemnation, to sustain alone, a weary but unyielding Atlas, the world that his own ideals have fashioned despite the trampling march of unconscious power.

MAN AND THE RACE [12]

By George Edward Woodberry

Professor Woodberry was for many years a teacher of literature at Columbia University. He is a poet as well. The following excerpt is taken from *The Torch*.

It belongs to a highly developed race to become, in a true sense, aristocratic—a treasury of its best in practical and spiritual types, and then to disappear in the surrounding tides of men. So Athens dissolved like a pearl in the cup of the Mediterranean, and Rome in the cup of Europe, and Judæa in the cup of the Universal Communion. Though death is the law of all life, man touches this earthen fact with the wand of the spirit, and transforms it into the law of sacrifice. Man has won no victory over his environment so sublime as this, finding in his mortal sentence the true choice of the soul and in the road out of Paradise the open highway of eternal life. Races die; but the ideal of sacrifice as the highest race-destiny has seldom occurred to men, though it has been suggested both by devout Jews and by devout Irishmen as the divinely appointed organic law of the Hebrew and the Celt. In the general view of men the

[12] Reprinted with the permission of Harcourt, Brace and Company.

extinction of a race partakes of the unreasoning finality of nature.

The vital flow of life has this in common with disease—that it is self-limited; the fever runs its course, and burns away. "All thoughts, all passions, all delights," have this history. In the large arcs of social being, movements of the human spirit, however embracing and profound, obey the same law of the limitation of specific energy. Revolutions, reforms, rebirths exhaust their fuel, and go out. Races are only greater units of man; for a race, as for an individual, there is a time to die; and that time, as history discloses it, is the moment of perfection. This is the largest fact in the moral order of the world; it is the center of providence in history. In the life of the human spirit the death of the best of its achieving elements, in the moment of their consummation, is as the fading of the flower of the field or the annual fall of the leaves of the forest in the natural world; and unless this be sacrificial death, it were wantonness and waste like the deaths of nature; but man and his works are supernatural, and raised above nature by an imperishable relation which they contain. Race-history is a perpetual celebration of the Mass. The Cross initials every page with its broad gold, and he whose eye misses that letter has lost the clew to the meaning. I do not refer to the self-devotion of individuals, the sacred lives of the race. I speak of the involuntary element in the life of nations, or what seems such on the vast scale of social life. Always some great culture is dying to enrich the soil of new harvests, some

civilization is crumbling to rubbish to be the hill of a
more beautiful city, some race is spending itself that a
lower and barbarous world may inherit its stored treas-
ure-house. Although no race may consciously devote
itself to the higher ends of mankind, it is the prerogative
of its men of genius so to devote it; nor is any nation
truly great which is not so dedicated by its warriors and
statesmen, its saints and heroes, its thinkers and dream-
ers. A nation's poets are its true owners; and by the
stroke of the pen they convey the title-deeds of its real
possessions to strangers and aliens.

This dedication of the energy of a race by its men
of genius to the higher ends of mankind is the sap of
all the world. The spiritual life of mankind spreads, the
spiritual unity of mankind grows, by this age-long surrender of privilege and power into the hands of the
world's new men, and the leavening of the mass by the
best that has anywhere arisen in it, which is thus
brought about. The absorption of aristocracies in democracies, the dissolution of the nobler product in
inferior environments, the salutary death of cultures,
civilizations, breeds of men, is the strict line on which
history, drawing the sundered parts of the earth slowly
together, moves to that great consummation when the
best that has at any time been in the world shall be the
portion of every man born into it. If the old English
blood, which here on this soil gave birth to a nation,
spread civilization through it, and cast the orbit of its
starry course in time, is destined to be thus absorbed
and lost in the nation which it has formed, we should be

proud and happy in such a fate; for this is to wear the
seal of God's election in history. Nay, if the aristocracy
of the whole white race is so to melt in a world of the
colored races of the earth, I for one should only rejoice
in such a divine triumph of the sacrificial idea in history; for it would mean the humanization of mankind.

Unless this principle is strongly grasped, unless there
be an imperishable relation in man and his works which
they contain, and which, though it has other phases, here
appears in this eternal salvage stored up in a slowly per-
fecting race, history through its length and breadth is
a spectacle to appall and terrify the reason. The perpetual flux of time—

"Scepters, tiaras, swords, and chains, and tomes
Of reasoned wrong, glozed on by ignorance"—

is a mere catastrophe of blood and error unless its
mighty subverting and dismaying changes are related to
something which does not pass away with dethroned
gods, abandoned empires, and repealed codes of law and
morals. But in the extinction of religions, in imperial
revolutions, in the bloody conflict of ideas, there is one
thing found stable; it is the mind itself, growing
through ages. That which in its continuity we call the
human spirit, abides. Men, tribes, states disappear, but
the race-mind endures. A conception of the world and
an emotional response thereto constitute the life of the
race-mind, and fill its consciousness with ideas and feelings, but in these there is no element of chance, con-
tingency, or frailty; they are master-ideas, master-

emotion, clothed with the power of a long reign over men, and imposing themselves upon each new generation almost with the yoke of necessity. What I designated as the race-mind—the sole thing permanent in history—is this potentiality of thought and feeling, in any age, realizing itself in states of mind and habits of action long established in the race, deeply inherited, and slowly modified. The race-mind is the epitome of the past. It contains all human energy, knowledge, experience, that survives. It is the resultant of millions of lives whose earthly power it stores in one deathless force. This race-mind is simply formed. Life presents certain permanent aspects in the environment, which generate ways of behavior thereto, normal and general among men. The world is a multiplicity, a harvest-field, a battle-ground; and thence arise through human contact ways of numbering, or mathematics, ways of tillage, or agriculture, ways of fighting, or military tactics and strategy, and these are incorporated in individuals as habits of life. The craftsman has the mind of his craft. Life also presents certain other permanent internal aptitudes in the soul, whence arises the mind of the artist, the inventor, the poet. But this cast of mind of the mathematician or of the painter is rather a phase of individual life. In the larger unit of the race, environment and aptitude, working together in the historic life of ages, develop ideas, moods, and energies characteristic of the race in which they occur. In the sphere of ideas, freedom is indissolubly linked with the English, righteousness with the Hebrew; in the temperamental sphere, a signal instance is the Celtic genius—mystery, twilight, supernatural fantasy, lamentation, tragic disaster; or the Greek genius—definiteness, proportioned beauty, ordered science, philosophic principle; and, in the sphere of energy, land and gold-hunger, and that strange soul-hunger—hunger to possess the souls of men—which is at the root of all propagandism, have been motive powers in many races.

Thus, in one part or another of time and place, and from causes within and without, the race, coming to its best, flowers in some creative hope, ripens in some shaping thought, glows in some resistless enthusiasm. Each of these in its own time holds an age in its grasp. They seize on men and shape them in multitudes to their will, as the wind drives the locusts; make men hideous ascetics, send them on forlorn voyages, devote them to the block and the stake, make Argonauts, Crusaders, Lollards of them, fill Europe in one age with a riot of revolution and in the next with the camps of tyrannic power. These ideas, moods, energies have mysterious potency; they seem to possess an independent being; though, like all the phenomena of life-energy, they are self-limited, the period of their growth, culmination, and decline extends through generations and centuries; they seem less the brood of man's mind than higher powers that feed on men. They are surrounded by a cloud of witnesses—fanatics, martyrs, dupes; they doom whole peoples to glory or shame; in the undying battle of the soul they are the choosers of the slain. Though they proceed from the human spirit, they rule it; and in life they are the spiritual presences which are most closely unveiled to the apprehension, devotion, and love of men.

The race-mind building itself from immemorial time out of this mystery of thought and passion, as generation after generation kneels and fights and fades, takes unerringly the best that anywhere comes to be in the world, holds to it with the cling of fate, and lets all else fall to oblivion; out of this best it has made, and still fashions, that enduring world of idea and emotion into which we are born as truly as into the natural world. It has a marvelous economy.

> "One accent of the Holy Ghost
> The heedless world has never lost."

Egypt, India, Greece and Rome, Italy, the English, France, America, the Turk, the Persian, the Russian, the Japanese, the Chinese, the Negro, feed its pure tradition of what excellence is possible to the race-mind, and has grown habitual in its being; and, as in the old myth, it destroys its parent, abolishing all these differences of climate, epoch, and skull. The race-mind unifies the race which it preserves; that is its irresistible line of advance. It wipes out the barriers of time, language, and country. It undoes the mischief of Babel, and restores to mankind one tongue in which all things can be understood by all men. It fuses the Bibles of all nations in one wisdom and one practice. It knocks off the tribal fetters of caste and creed; and, substituting thought for blood as the bond of the world, it slowly liberates that free soul, which is one in all men and common to all mankind. To free the soul in the individual life, and to accomplish the unity of mankind—that is its work. . . .

It is obvious that what I have advanced brings the principle of authority into a cardinal place in life, and clothes tradition with great power. It might seem that the individual in becoming one with the race-mind has only to endue himself with the past as with a garment, to take its mold with the patience of clay, and to be in the issue a recast of the past, thinking old thoughts, feeling old emotions, doing old actions, in preëstablished ways. But this is to misconceive the process by which the individual effects this union; he does not take the impress of the race-mind as the wax receives the imprint of the seal. This union is an act of life, a process of energy, joy, and growth, of self-expression; here learning is living, and there is no other way to know the doctrine than to do its will; so the race-mind is not copied, but is perpetually reborn in men, and the world which each one of us thus builds for himself out of his preferred capacities, memories, and desires—our farmer's, engineer's, painter's world, as I have said—is his own original and unique world. There is none like it, none. Originality consists in this rebirth of the world in the young soul. This world, nevertheless, the world of each of us, is not one of willfulness, fantasy, and caprice; if, on the one hand, it is such stuff as dreams are made of, on the other it is the stuff of necessity. It has a consistency, a law and fate, of its own, which supports, wields, and sustains it. Authority is no more than the recognition of and obedience to this underlying principle of being, whose will is disclosed to us in man's life so far as that life in its wholeness falls within our view; in knowledge of this will all wisdom consists, of its action in us all experience is woven, and in union with it all private judgment is confirmed. Authority, truly interpreted, is only another phase of that identity of the soul in all men by virtue of which society exists, and especially that intellectual state arises, that state which used to be called the republic of letters and which is the institution of the race-mind to be the center, the home and hope of civilization in all ages—that state where the unity of mankind is accomplished in the spiritual unities of science, art, and love.

To sum up these suggestions which I have thought it desirable to offer in order that the point of view taken in these lectures might, perhaps, be plain, I conceive of history as a single process in which through century after century in race after race the soul of man proceeds in a progressive comprehension of the universe and evolution of its own humanity, and passes on to each new generation its accumulated knowledge and developed energies, in their totality and without loss, at the acme of achievement. I conceive of this inheriting and bequeathing power as having its life and action in the race-mind. I conceive of literature as an organ of the race-mind, and of education as the process by which the individual enters into the race-mind, becomes more and more man, and in the spiritual life mainly by means of literature. I conceive of the body of men who thus live and work in the soul as constituting the intellectual state, that republic of letters, in which the race-mind reaches, from age to age, its maximum of knowledge and power, in men of genius and those whose lives they illumine, move, and direct; the unity of mankind is the ideal end of this state, and the freeing of the soul which takes place in it is its means. I conceive of the progressive life of this state, in civilization after civilization, as a perpetual death of the best, in culture after culture, for the good of the lower, a continuing sacrifice, in the history of humanity, of man for mankind. And from this mystery, though to some it may seem only the recourse of intellectual despair, I pluck a confident faith in that imperishable relation which man and his works contain, and which though known only in the continuity of the race-mind, I am compelled to believe, has eternal reality.

THE PERMANENT WITHIN THE FLUX [18]

By Paul Elmer More

The Victorian age, even more than others, was a time of transition. It has passed, and one thing at least is sure: we shall have no great literature again until we have looked once more within our own breasts and learned that there is something in human nature besides an *indefinite congeries of changes*. As it is now, the

[18] Reprinted from the essay, "Victorian Literature," in *Shelburne Essays*, Seventh Series, with the permission of the publishers, the Houghton Mifflin Company.

very mold and *genre* of the higher emotion have been
lost. It is almost inconceivable, for example, that a true
tragedy should be composed today; for the tragic character, whether it be Antigone breaking herself mag-
nanimously in the name of the unwritten eternal laws
against the edicts of Creon, or Œdipus bruised and
blinded by his ignorance of the divine purpose but
caught up after years of submission into mystic fellowship with the gods, or Hamlet musing undecided while
he listens to the fateful voices—everywhere the tragic
mood depends on the unresolved conflict in human
motives between the universal and the particular, the
changeless law and the temporal passion. It even seems
that, with the disappearance of the greater form, there
is passing away the ambition to write greatly. And
naturally. For if the permanence of a work of art is
due to its fit expression of the permanent in human
desire and experience, what room is there for the long
hope, or what impulse to sacrifice present popularity for
enduring fame, when the very notion has become dis-
credited of any principle contrary to ceaseless change?

I have been concerned here primarily with literature,
but obviously the destiny of literature is bound up with
that of the practical world. If the disregard of permanence means formlessness and the absence of the higher
emotion in letters, it means the same thing in society;
nor under the existing worship of change, whether
economic theory follows the individualism of Cobden
or the collectivism of Karl Marx, can there be any
escape for civilization from the present dominance of

material forces. Relax those brutal bulwarks against the inrush of ungoverned change, and the result is simple anarchy. Nor is there real hope from the mitigating influence of that humanitarian sympathy which has accompanied the growth of scientific intellectualism; for such sympathy is but another aspect of the same absorption in change, being an attempt of the individual to flow, so to speak, in the direction of every emotional impact from the world. It contains no power of resistance or principle of restraint, but tends on the contrary to make man a more helpless prey of the ever-encroaching flood. The only salvation is in the recognition of some superior guiding and dividing law of just rule and right subordination, in the perception, that is, of something permanent within the flux.

There is need of firm hearts and clear brains to bring us out of this slough of indifference, but unfortunately the strong men are too often paralyzed by a curious superstition of words. The saying has gone abroad that strength means joy in change and that he who would question change is reactionary and effeminate; and so in the name of progress and virility we drift supinely with the current. If by reactionary is understood only the man who shudders at all innovation and who cries out for some impossible restoration of the past, the charge is well made. Such a man in the social realm corresponds to the metaphysician who would deny the existence of change and the many for an exclusive and sterile idealism of the one. But reaction may be, and in the true sense is, something utterly different from this futile dreaming; it is essentially to answer action with action, to oppose to the welter of circumstance the force of discrimination and selection, to direct the aimless tide of change by reference to the co-existing law of the immutable fact, to carry the experience of the past into the diverse impulses of the present, and so to move forward in an orderly progression. If any young man, feeling now within himself the power of accomplishment, hesitates to be called a reactionary, in this better use of the term, because of the charge of effeminacy, let him take courage. The world is not contradicted with impunity, and he who sets himself against the world's belief will have need of all a man's endurance and all a man's strength. The adventurous soul who today against the reigning scientific and pragmatic dogma would maintain no vague and equally one-sided idealism, but the true duality of the one and the many, the absolute and the relative, the permanent and the mutable, will find himself subjected to an intellectual isolation and contempt almost as terrible as the penalties of the Inquisition, and quite as effective in producing a silent conformity. If a man doubts this, let him try, and learn. Submission to the philosophy of change is the real effeminacy; it is the virile part to react.

DISCUSSION AND THEME TOPICS

1. After thoughtful consideration of the following points, write down your answers and comments as indicated:
   a. If you could have been given your choice in the world's history as to the period in which you should live your life, what century, past, present,

or future, would you have selected? Why? Set
down, if you can, the conditions which make for
human happiness and welfare, and show how they
came nearer being realized in the age which you
have chosen than in any other.

b. What particular elements in civilization have
reached their highest point of development in our
own age? (These might be factors connected either
with man himself or with his environment.) Are
these factors among those which you have chosen
as the source of the happiness of mankind?

c. What elements in our civilization are evidently not
at the highest point in their evolution? Perhaps
they have even entered upon the process of decay.
What was the golden age for each of these particular factors? What evidence have you that, in
these respects, we are in a period of retrogression?

d. Is there any evidence available in the universe, or
in its history, that there is progress toward some
ultimate attainment that is good?

e. Do you believe that man's residence upon the earth,
now a matter of some thousands of years' duration,
is to go on indefinitely? If not, what conditions
might possibly bring his existence to a close?

f. When the whole thing is at last over and done
with, when the curtain has dropped upon the final
act, would you call the play worth enacting?

2. Consider yourself a reporter to whom has been assigned
the task of interviewing some distinguished man in a
particular field upon the idea of progress. The article
which you write, we will suppose, is to appear in some
one of the monthly magazines. By your questions you
are to invite from your scholar expression of opinion
and comment upon points of particular interest and significance. It will be necessary for you to study the topic
which you select and to arrange the questions and comment in some logical sequence:

a. The Doctor Looks at the Idea of Progress.

Here, of course, the discussion will have to do

largely with the physical side of man and animals. Questions of bodily structure, complexity of form and function, adaptation, resistance to disease, deterioration, and degradation, will be considered, and some conclusion arrived at. Psychological considerations will be pertinent in the case of man.

b. The Physicist Looks at the Idea of Progress.

Man is but an episode in the history of the universe, appearing at a time favorable to his existence, doomed to disappear when such conditions no longer exist. The history of the solar universe, the sequence of geologic ages on our planet, the evolution and devolution of plant and animal life, and their final extinction—these will be points of interest.

c. The Idealist Looks at the Idea of Progress.

The Idealist will probably be some one who believes in progress towards some "far-off divine event toward which the whole creation moves," blindly, stumblingly, and often with false steps which have to be retraced, but *on*, inevitably *on*. The perfectibility of mankind is the central point of his doctrine. The Idealist may be a religionist, who places faith in a Divine Power controlling human destiny, or a champion of some economic or social theory, or a believer, like Rousseau, in the innate and original goodness of man. Visualize your character clearly and then let him talk.

d. The Philosopher of Pessimism Looks at the Idea of Progress.

This man will be one whose study of the universe and of man has forced him to renounce all hope for the betterment of mankind or of his condition on this planet, or even for his extended existence here. If he ever had hope, he is now the victim of his disillusionment, and his philosophy becomes one of stoical endurance or of Epicurean indulgence.

3. The following charges are not infrequently brought

against the present era. If you feel that some of this criticism is made without justification, present a well-reasoned defense of your generation, with supporting evidence. It would be well to center your attention upon one or two closely related points:

Points of criticism of our time:

a. That it is a "jazz age."
b. That it is not a beautiful age.
c. That it is an age of disillusionment and repudiation.
d. That it is a materialistic and sordid age.
e. That it is a hectic and sensuous age.
f. That it is not a reflective age.
g. That the age has lost its sense of honor, high chivalry, and capacity for devotion to a cause.

4. The poet Keats said:

> Beauty is truth, truth beauty—that is all
> Ye know on earth, and all ye need to know.

Some one else has declared that he for one needed to know a great deal more. Do you consider devotion to beauty a sufficient guide to living? Write out a statement of your ideas in this regard. Read "Wanted: A Substitute for Righteousness," by Avis Carlson, in *Harper's Magazine*, January, 1927, an article already referred to in Chapter III.

5. Read John Masefield's little poem "Cargoes," and take from it a suggestion for a discussion of relative beauty in different periods of the world's history.

SUGGESTIONS FOR MORE EXTENDED STUDY

1. Read somewhat widely among the essays of Agnes Repplier as found in *Counter-Currents*, *Points of Friction*, *Under Dispute*, and see if you can discover her working philosophy of life.

2. Read Robert Shafer's *Progress and Science* and analyze in a critical paper his conception of the value of science in the development of civilization.

3. Read the little books of Ralph Adams Cram listed in the bibliography and write a critical discussion of his "mediaevalism."

4. Read David Grayson's *Adventures in Contentment* and Charles Wagner's *The Simple Life* and discuss the sources of satisfaction which these writers find rewarding.

5. Make a study of the social philosophy of H. G. Wells as set forth in the closing chapter of his *Outline of History* and in his book, *The Salvaging of Civilization*. Where does he place his hope for social betterment?

VOCABULARY LIST

decadence
macrocosm
rejuvenated
fortitude
precursor
Antichrist
veritable
millennium
auspices
gloating
determinism
teleology
implicit
parasite
naturalism
palinode
votaries
gird
cataclysm
apocalyptic
priority
collocation
oblivion
impact
virile
encroaching

aggregate
apprehend
secularism
amelioration
vouchsafe
nacre
Utopia
rhapsodist
planetary
glibly
intimated
pertinacity
insatiable
feckless
sterile
inertia
doctrinaire
equilibrium
innovation
sundry
collaboration
epitome
congeries
flux
supinely

obloquy
inalienable
cynic
proletariat
bourgeoisie
régime
obliviscence
prototype
wistful
Machiavellian
enervating
indubitable
dilemma
orthodox
panacea
chronic
fission
cohesion
clique
débâcle
atrophied
ascetic
genre
Inquisition
collectivism

READING LIST

The list comprises the sources from which the excerpts in the text are taken, and other works bearing upon the discussion of the chapter.

William Ralph Inge. *Outspoken Essays*, Second Series. London, 1922.
Ralph Adams Cram. *The Decadent*. 1893. Privately printed.
——*Nemesis of Mediocrity*. 1917.
——*The Great Thousand Years*. 1918.
——*The Sins of the Fathers*. 1919.
——*Walled Towns*. Boston, 1919.
Albert E. Wiggam. *The New Decalogue of Science*. Indianapolis, 1923.
——*The Fruit of the Family Tree*. Indianapolis, 1924.
Henry L. Mencken and Robert R. LaMonte. *Men Versus the Man*. New York, 1910.
Harold E. Stearns. *The Intellectual Life*. (See Chapter IV.)
Charles A. Bennett. *At a Venture*. New York, 1924.
Charles H. Grandgent. *Old and New*. Cambridge, 1920.
Agnes Repplier. *Points of Friction*. Boston, 1920.
——*Under Dispute*. Boston, 1924.
Walter Lippmann. *Drift and Mastery*. New York, 1914.
André Siegfried. *America Comes of Age*. New York, 1927.
Bertrand Russell. *Mysticism and Logic*.
George E. Woodberry. *The Torch*. New York, 1905.
Elmer More. *Shelburne Essays*. Seventh Series. Boston,
——Eighth Series. Boston, 1913. (Chapter on Walter

——fer. *Progress and Science*. New Haven, 1922.
——illikan. *Science and Life*. Boston, 1926.
——*e Idea of Progress*. London, 1920.
——Holmes. *New Churches for Old*. New York,

——dson. *The Truths We Live By*. New York,

——t. *What Men Live By*. Boston, 1914.

Charles W. Eliot. *Durable Satisfactions of Life.* New York, 1910.

——*Training for an Effective Life.*

Walter Pater. *Marius, the Epicurean.*

University of Chicago Professors. *The Nature of the World and of Man.* Chicago, 1926.

Lewis Mumford. *The Golden Day.* New York, 1926.

Ulysses G. Weatherly. *Social Progress; Studies in the Dynamics of Change.*

H. G. Wells. *The Salvaging of Civilization.* New York, 1921.

Edgar A. Singer. *Modern Thinkers and Present Problems.* New York, 1923.

Edward Carpenter. *Civilization: Its Cause and Cure.* New York, 1897.